STOPS

ALONG

THE

COUNTRY

ROAD

STOPS ALONG THE COUNTRY ROAD

by
Fr. Joseph Breighner

Cathedral Foundation Press
Baltimore, Maryland

Printed and bound in the United States of America.

2 3 4 5   05 04 03 02 01 00 99 98 97

ISBN 1-885938-03-9

Library of Congress Cataloging-in-Publication Data

Breighner, Joseph.
    Stops along the country road / by Joseph Breighner.
        p.   cm.
    "New "Father Joe" book spun from syndicated radio show."--CIP galley.
    ISBN 1-885938-03-9   (pbk. : alk. paper)
    1. Christian life--Catholic authors. 2. Christian life--Anecdotes
    3. Christian life--Humor. 4. Country music--History and criticism.
    5. Breighner, Joseph. I. Country Road (Radio program) II. Title.
    BX2350.2.B685   1996
    248.4'82--dc20   96-15862
                                     CIP

Published in 1996 by

Cathedral Foundation Press
P.O. Box 777
Baltimore, Maryland 21203

Publisher: Daniel L. Medinger
Press Director: Gregg A. Wilhelm
Assistant Manager: Patti Medinger
Book design: Sue Seiler
Cover design: Steven Fabijanski
Frontcover photograph: Denise Walker
Backcover photograph: Gregg A. Wilhelm

Contents

Forewords

Stops along the country road. It's not Dorothy's yellow brick road. It's not route sixty-six sprawling across the continental USA. It's surely not the autobahn. It's a simple country road filled with music and the thoughts such music evokes. Our companion and guide along this road is Fr. Joe Breighner—priest, psychologist, disc jockey.

Maybe it's a listener from the mid-west or the south, and while their accents isolate the part of the country they're calling from, their request is universally the same. "I'd like to have a copy of 'The Country Road' program ...," and then they say a number. Someone in this vast space known as radioland has heard Father Joe. More importantly, what he said touched their hearts, and the singed moment of mutual awareness is something they want to touch—or rather, hear—again and again.

People like Fr. Joe Breighner—people who use the radio to preach the gospel of Jesus Christ—have enormous faith. They create program after program not knowing exactly who's out there listening. Not knowing whether anyone truly cares. Using language that makes the gospel easy to understand. That's the faith part. It is difficult preaching the gospel without having any human reaction when the program is aired, unlike a preacher who can look upon the expressive faces of his congregation. Weeks later, a radio priest like Father Joe might get a letter (wonderful letters) or a phone call comes to our offices at Paulist Communications (heartwarming phone calls) saying that they want copies of

Father Joe's scripts or that they would like to order a cassette tape of one of his programs. Does a letter mean one listener or a thousand? Radio experts can't really say. There's that faith again.

So, why do it? Because St. Paul challenges us. "How will they hear, unless someone preaches?" Because Pope Paul VI told us that, if we are to be good evangelizers, we must adapt the gospel to the language of the people.

Father Joe Breighner does that repeatedly week after week on radio. "The Country Road" isn't just a radio program. It isn't just the most popular country-formatted religious radio program in the United States. It's a vessel that Father Joe uses to bring people to love Jesus in a way that he hopes will lead them to follow Jesus as Christians and as Catholics.

So, Father Joe is a priest and a psychologist and a disc jockey. But, more importantly, he's an imitator—an imitator of Jesus Christ who came preaching the good news of God's love for all human kind. And that makes Father Joe an evangelizer.

In the book you're about to read, in these edited versions of his scripts, you'll begin to see why Father Joe touches so many people to whom he speaks on the radio. And you'll also know why at the end of all of the country roads, there's an encounter with this person Jesus whose way of life leads each of us to a deeper understanding of who we are, who God is, and how we are connected to God by our love for those around us.

It's a wonderful journey.

John Geaney, CSP
Silver Spring, Maryland
May, 1996

The best way to express my involvement with Father Joe and "The Country Road" would be to paraphrase the old Hair Club for Men slogan, "I'm not only the producer, but also a fan."

My first broadcasting job was at a small radio station that aired country music with a lot of religious programming in the early morning and weekend hours. Having been raised (and schooled) in a Catholic environment, I had very little exposure to the teachings and perspectives of other Christian denominations or different religious beliefs. So imagine my surprise when I discovered that a couple of these "religious" shows focused on topics that had very little to do with Christian faith and living. A few programs almost had me convinced that the world was about to end *real* soon. (This was almost twenty years ago!)

Most, however, were quite true to form in providing inspiration and guidance, but something was missing. I did not realize exactly what it was until a few years later when I started working at WPOC in Baltimore and discovered Fr. Joe Breighner's "The Country Road," a half-hour show airing twice on Sundays. Here was this Catholic priest actually speaking in a conversational manner about real life day-to-day issues, interwoven with country music and some pretty corny jokes (many of which I have, um, "borrowed"). How refreshing!

In 1982, my personal life took a downward turn, leaving me with a crisis of confidence and very low self-esteem. It was at that point that I started listening to "The Country Road" a little more intently. What amazed me was that this priest, who I barely knew at the time, seemed to know so much about my problems. I remember during one particular show saying out loud to myself, over and over again, "How'd he know that?" I took great comfort in realizing, through weekly trips with "The Country Road," that my problems were not that unusual for someone in my situation. I was hooked!

I finally met Father Joe two years later, at the radio station's Christmas party, and could not get over the fact that he was always joking, always smiling. Up until that point, my only encounters with priests were in Mass, confession, and in school, when the Monsignor would come into each class and dole out report cards. (Talk about seeing a *lack* of smiles.)

In the fall of 1986, the disc jockey responsible for producing "The Country Road" left WPOC. That meant, until someone was hired for that particular airshift, which included producing "The Country Road" as a duty, Father Joe had to grab whoever was available and/or willing to work the booth when it came time to record. On one special day, I happened to be in the front lobby when Father Joe arrived. The chief engineer was scheduled to record the programs (usually two per session). I politely asked if I could sit in and learn the ropes. The chief engineer was more than happy to have me along. Not only did he teach me how to produce the show, but he also allowed me to go ahead and do it. At that point, I realized that as long as I was employed by WPOC, Father Joe would never have to worry about finding someone to produce "The Country Road."

This new responsibility allowed me to be directly involved with one of the best programs of its kind. As the new producer, I immediately realized as good as the content of "The Country Road" was (and still is, after twenty incredible years on the air), the quality of production at that time lacked something. So, with Father Joe's permission, I have implemented various changes over the years, such as a revised recording process that makes for a tighter sounding show; switching from vinyl records to CDs for the show's musical interludes; and, more recently, producing the show completely on a digital workstation. Granted, most of these changes have resulted in a bit more effort on my part to produce an entire program, but it is a labor of love—a kind of payback for the reassurance received from Father Joe and "The Country Road" in my time of need.

Over the years, my work on "The Country Road" has been rewarding not only professionally, but also on a more personal level. My friendship with Father Joe has grown to the point where I consider him as an older brother. Equally rewarding is knowing that through listening to "The Country Road," many others also share this feeling.

Tony Girard
Baltimore, Maryland
May, 1996

Introduction

"Sleeping single in a double bed..."

The words of Barbara Mandrell's song echoed in my ears. They seemed like a description of my life. I kept waiting for someone to walk into the studio and say, "What's a nice priest like you doing in a place like this?"

The "place" is the place I've been for more than twenty years—the studio of WPOC, Baltimore's top-rated country music radio station. For these many years I have spent one night a week listening to country music, jotting down lyrics and making notes in the margins of paper while preparing my weekly radio show, "The Country Road."

I'm not sure what hell is like, but listening to country music love songs while trying to live a celibate life has to be close. Listening to Kenny Rogers' song "Morning Desire," while knowing all that I had to look forward to in the morning was the newspaper, is not my idea of a good time. Yet, this is what I assigned myself to do. How did I ever get into this mess?

It began innocently enough when I answered the telephone one day at St. Charles Church in Pikesville, a northwestern suburb of the city, where I was an associate pastor. The caller was Pete Porter, a former sportscaster for a local television station, who announced that he was now program director at WPOC.

"Have you heard of WPOC?" he asked. He might have well asked if I ever visited the dark side of the moon.

"No, I haven't," I said.

Pete explained that the station just hit the airwaves a few months earlier. The crew was trying to develop an ecumenical religious program with visiting priests, ministers, and rabbis as commentators. He asked if I'd be interested. Being young, daring, and somewhat self-destructive, I agreed.

Only one minister and I showed up for taping that first week in 1975. The format consisted of two-minute commentaries on the quarter hour between six and eight o'clock on Sunday mornings. In between our commentaries, disk jockeys played country gospel music. As I listened to music that I never heard before I began to think that I really was on the dark side of the moon! This particular format was so unappealing that not one other priest, minister, or rabbi ever showed up to provide commentary. While the different believers of the world's religions could not agree on matters of faith, they could agree on matters of music—they hated country!

By the third week of taping, the other minister said he could no longer do the show. Embarrassingly, I have forgotten his name. I hope he reads this and calls me. I want to shake his hand again, and congratulate him on his good judgment. His departure left me on my own. I faced the inevitable that the end was near. But, a firm believer in life after death, I talked again to Pete.

"Pete," I said, "this is a terrible format. Only my mother listens to the program. Even I don't like it. Instead of using gospel music, how about inserting commentary around the current 'Top 40' of country music, around the music and themes people hear everyday?"

Pete seemed perplexed, so I phrased my idea in a single sentence: "I want to create a religious show for people who hate religious shows!"

I argued that for God to be believable in every day life I had to relate him to the things people experienced in every day life.

Peter just smiled and said, "I'm not sure what you mean, but if you prepare a script, we'll tape it and see where it goes from there."

I made a bold assertion of how the show should be done, but there was one problem: I knew virtually nothing about country music. A product of the 1950s, rock was "in" during my adolescent years and country was "out." In fact, we even kind of looked down on people who listened to country music. We were the cool, hip, "with it" rockers and country listeners were square, straight-laced, and "out of it." I grew up in Middle River just east of Baltimore. Others around town looked down on people from this hard working, industrial, middle-class borough, so it was nice to be able to look down on someone else, namely the country music lovers.

I knew as much about country music as my grandmother knew about skeet shooting, which is to say "zilch." What knowledge I possessed was restricted to a line in a song heard years before: "I'm not mad at you because you're only chicken feed. I'm just mad at you because I'm not the only chicken you feed." With lyrics like that, who couldn't be converted?

I immersed myself in learning country music the way one might learn a foreign language. I spent hours each day tuned to the station, listening to the lyrics, feeling emotions from the instruments, zeroing in on the themes. For my early shows, I averaged about twenty hours of preparation a week for a thirty minute program. All my life I preached conversion; now I had to experience conversion!

To pick the right songs and reach the station's audience with my messages, I had to learn to like the music and love the people who listened to the music. Learning to love the listeners was easy, since loving people was what attracted me to the ministry. Learning to like the music turned out to be fun.

It became obvious that two basic qualities of country music was its playfulness and its earthiness. Country music is playful in that it laughs at itself. I'm convinced that some musicians write the title before they write the song. For example, it soon becomes apparent that the Kendalls' song "The Pittsburgh Stealers" is not about a football team. While the theme of infidelity is no laughing matter, there is a sense that the band is having fun as well as making a point. Country music is earthy because it embraces our deepest feelings and emotions: love, anger, jealousy, revenge, family, fidelity, disloyalty, and the list goes on. While the rhythm and beat may not appeal to everyone, the message is real to everyone. I sometimes call country music "soap operas in song."

Working with these earthy themes enables me to find a key into people's hearts. Too often institutionalized religion fails people because it judges people without trying to understand them. Rather than start with God and tell people they should measure up, I prefer to start with people and let them know that God is where they are, and God has a better way to live. By starting with people's needs, I hope to help them believe that God cares.

Whenever I think of judging others, I recall a true story that the great radio and television preacher Bishop Fulton Sheen once told. Bishop Sheen was riding on a subway one day in New York, when a disreputable looking gentleman, reeking of booze and b.o., entered the car and plopped down next to him. The man's eyes were glassy and he seemed to be just staring at a newspaper he held in his hands.

Finally, he turned to the Bishop and asked, "How does a man get diabetes?"

Figuring this was his chance, Bishop Sheen responded, "A man gets diabetes from drinking too much, and neglecting his wife and children!"

As soon as the words left his mouth, the bishop felt terrible. "I shouldn't have put the man down," he thought to himself.

In an effort to restart the conversation, Bishop Sheen asked, "Why did you ask that question about diabetes?"

The man replied, "Well, I was just reading here that the pope has diabetes."

Only a man as humble as Bishop Sheen would have revealed that story about himself. Life sometimes teaches us what country music already knows: we need to laugh at ourselves from time to time.

What's my rationale for using country music as a springboard for religious messages? How can I find sacred themes in secular music? Basically, I do not find easy distinctions between the sacred and the secular. I think all of life is sacred, and that God is involved with us, even when we may not be consciously involved with God. A "cheatin'" song about infidelity, for example, offers a wonderful opportunity for exploring how infidelity is destructive of self and of others. In other words, if we start with where people are, we can always help them see where they can be. I believe that was what Jesus did in his entire ministry. He was criticized for hanging out with sinners, publicans, and prostitutes, but only by being with them could he uplift them.

Essentially, by using music that sings about life, I attempt to do no more than what Jesus did in his parables about life. Jesus told stories that the people of his day could relate to and understand. He spoke of fishermen and farmers, of housewives and householders, of robbers and repentant sons. Jesus was down to earth, even earthy. He used spittle and clay to cure a blind man. He used salty language, such as his words to Peter "Get behind me Satan" (which we might translate differently in today's slang) and his reference to religious leaders as "illegitimate sons of Abraham" (which we would certainly translate differently in today's slang!).

When the lyrics of some songs are a bit rough around the edges, I think they are simply a reflection of life. If we are afraid to get dirty getting close to people who are earthy, I fear we have come a long way from the beginnings of Christianity. On this point, a priest friend once said to me, "The advantage of working with country music is that you'll never have to worry about being called in for heresy. No one in the hierarchy will ever admit that he listens to country music."

There are thousands of country music songs, but as I see it there are only five main themes: cheating, hurting, drinking, falling out of love, and falling in love. The novelist Willa Cather once noted that "there are only two or three stories in life, but they go on repeating themselves endlessly." That's a near perfect description of country music.

"Cheating" is the country term for infidelity. While infidelity is often sung about, it is rarely glorified. Lyrics may capture the passion, but they also capture the problem. Songs like Crystal Gayle's "Here I Go Down That Wrong Road Again" crystallize, pun intended, the reality of cheating, but it does not pretend to make a "wrong" a "right." I think that is one of the redemptive aspects of country music. It unveils the frailty of human behavior, but does not attempt to justify it. A line from Cal Smith's country classic—"The Lord knows I'm drinking and running around, but he don't need your loud mouth informing the town"—offers a great opportunity to relate country music to scripture. In the scene where the elders want to stone the woman caught in adultery, Jesus does not defend the sin, but he defends the sinner. He lets us know that the hypocrite is no better than the adulterer. Country music often packs this same kind of message.

The themes of hurting and falling out of love often go hand-in-hand and can be treated together here. No music on earth does a better job of describing hurt than country music. Since much of the hurt results from lost love, the two themes are often inseparable. In many songs, the drink and the jukebox are the working man's psychiatrist. Neither, however, solves any problem. As I say so often on the air, "The thing wrong with drowning our problems is that our problems learn how to swim." Songs like Mickey Gilley's "The Power Of Positive Drinking" open the door for me to suggest that positive thinking solves more problems than drinking!

Again, the beauty of wrapping messages around the music is that I can first identify with people's feelings before offering a possible solution. Falling out of love, for example, is a very common phenomenon given the increasing rate of divorce. On the topic of fading marriage, comedienne Phyllis Diller once commented, "I have a glowworm marriage; the glow is gone, but the worm remains." It's important when commenting on the music to help people differentiate feelings from love, so that they realize that love has not disappeared just because some romantic feelings are no longer present in a relationship. So many divorces could be prevented if we would just help people identify their unrealistic expectations of love and marriage. Who couldn't rekindle love in their relationship by listening to a warm, sentimental ballad called "I May Be Used, But Baby I Ain't Used Up"?

Drinking is another favorite theme in country music. For all the talk of drugs being such an epidemic, alcohol is the primary drug of choice. The drinking songs are perfect lead-ins to help people see the consequences of alcohol abuse, and that while booze is powerful, there is a Higher Power. I constantly emphasize that we can change, we can be different, we can un-learn bad habits. Too often in country music there is an implied fatalism that surrenders to the incorrect notion that things just happen and we can't do much about it. Highway 101's song "Whisky, If You Were A Woman" is about a woman who believes she can compete with another woman for her man's attention, but she can't compete with a bottle. Each of us is responsible for our behavior and each of us can change—with the help of God.

The falling-in-love songs celebrate romance and celebrate life. In country music there are many loves. There is a love for cars and the open highway. There is a love for simpler times. There is love, of course, for momma. A Mother's Day broadcast of "The Country Road" would be incomplete without Johnny Paycheck's "I'm The Only Hell My Momma Ever Raised." There is also love for Sundays in the South, and for trains and children and animals. After all, country music is essentially about sentimentality and the ways of the heart. If there is fatalism in the hurting songs, there is surely celebration in the love songs. I always select one of the love songs to end the show, which emphasizes that love not hate, healing not hurting, life not death has the last word.

Over the years on "The Country Road," I have discussed literally hundreds of topics and used thousands of songs. Boil the show down though, and it is not about themes so much as it is just one person talking to another. Each half hour consists of six or seven songs totalling about twenty minutes of music and another ten minutes of me chatting in between them. My approach is not "the wise person talking to people in need," but one struggling person trying to help another struggling person. I like the image of the wounded healer. All of us suffer wounds. We get hurt by life. Our experiences of pain either make us bitter or better people. We can decide to become bitter and retire into a state of cynicism. Or we can allow pain to make us better, make us more sensitive to the pain of others, and thereby interested in helping each other.

Ultimately, the show is not at all about country music. It is about life. While I use the music to get people's attention, most of my commentary between songs stands independent of the music. Jesus used parables to make his points, but the moral was more important than the story. I try to use country music in a similar way. Hopefully, my comments help others to work through their feelings and problems. For the person drinking too much, I want him or her to know there is a way to stop. For the woman crying over her husband's infidelity, I want her to know that God has not been unfaithful and is with her still. For the person hurting and feeling alone, I want him to know that someone cares. For the couple struggling to keep their marriage together, I want them to know that love is a decision, and that fidelity and commitment are worthy ideals.

"We'll see where it goes from there," Pete Porter said back in 1975. From there "The Country Road" has gone on for twenty years and is syndicated to almost one hundred stations around the country and in Guam.

Gathered here is a hodgepodge of scripts aired over the years. They have been grouped and edited to explore common themes to which we all can relate: life and how to deal with it; loss and how to handle it; language and how what we say makes others feel; love and how to keep it or how to move on when it's gone. Love—God's precious gift to us and our delicate gift to one another—is what each piece is ultimately about.

Since this book is a compilation of scripts, a few song titles are repeated throughout these pages. Die-hard fans might want to seek out some of the tunes I refer to and give them a listen. However, it should be noted, you don't need to be an encyclopedia of country music knowledge, or even a fan of country music, to understand and benefit from my messages. If this book does indeed make a country music convert out of you, well that's just an added blessing!

Stitches of humor thread throughout these pieces. A good sense of humor, I think, is crucial to a healthful, joyful, and gratifying life. Laughter should be packed away as part of everyone's survival kit. The book's middle section, "Laughter," is a short potpourri of funny lists culled from my columns that appear weekly in *The Catholic Review*. I thank the publisher for permission to reprint them here.

Thanks also to the friends and fine staff at WPOC in Baltimore for letting me take over the airwaves once a week, and especially Tony Girard who has produced "The Country Road" for the last ten years. Thanks, too, to Fr. John Geaney, CSP, president of Paulist Communications, which syndicates the show.

In choosing "The Country Road" as the title of my show, I wished to convey that life is a journey. I like the notion that we are all pilgrims traveling the road of life. One of my favorite scripture passages is the story of Jesus walking with two disciples along the road to Emmaus. One of the lines in John Denver's "Country Roads," which I adopted as the show's theme song, is "radio reminds me of my home far away." We are pilgrims on a journey through life to a distant place, a peaceful city, a state of eternal joy. Our destination lies in the distance, but God is never far away from us. God is someone right along with us who is trying to help. God is the friend at our side, the good shepherd carrying us through dark valleys, the light shining through darkness. Life is too long to walk alone. Life is just long enough when we walk together.

So now take a moment and pull over to the shoulder of life, and join me for a stop along the country road.

LIFE

Hoping and Healing
Along the Way

COUNTRY VALUES

♪

Neal McCoy
"The City Put The Country Back In Me"

As we think about living country values in a city setting, we realize what Neal McCoy sings in "The City Put The Country Back In Me" is true: we "don't have to leave our roots." Life is about having roots, which doesn't mean being stuck in the past. It means being grounded in some set of values that gives direction to our lives—past, present, and future. Such direction doesn't have to be real complicated.

"Love God with your whole heart and soul, and love your neighbor as yourself," Jesus said. "Those two commandments fulfill the law and the prophets." In two sentences, Jesus summed up most of our moral traditions. Values are not all that complicated. Living values can be the tough part, especially in a society that rejects or contradicts these values. And yet, if we are honest, it would be so much harder living without values. Imagine a world without the ten commandments. Imagine a world without some general agreement that killing, stealing, and adultery are wrong. Sure, these commandments are often broken, but at least we know they are commandments.

Occasionally, young couples ask me about raising children. Some say that they don't want to raise their children in any particular tradition or denomination so that the children will be free to choose their own faith when they grow up. My usual response is that if we give our children no faith to believe in, they may simply grow up thinking faith is unimportant. By raising them in a particular religious tradition, they at least have a basis for making decisions. Our values can mature—for example, from not killing someone to loving our enemies—but a foundational set of values is required before we can grow toward a more developed set of values.

When I think of the confusion surrounding values today, and Neal McCoy's song about finding a country bar in the city, I recall the story of two men at a pub. One asked the man next to him, "Are you from Ireland?" "I am," the second man replied. "Did you go to St. Brendan's school?" the first man asked. "I did," replied the second. "Did you have Sister Angela as your teacher in the third grade?" asked the first man. "I did," replied the second. "What amazing coincidences," the first man concluded. Someone overhearing the conversation asked the bartender what it was all about. The bartender replied, "Pay no attention to them. It's the Kelly twins. They're drunk again."

Tim McGraw
"Down On The Farm"

These days, there are probably more songs about farms than there are people who actually live on farms. Yet, the songs and the memories are of people and times when it was okay to have fun, to enjoy each other's company without sex being the basis of every relationship, a time when working hard was balanced by playing hard. Winning is not the most important thing. Those kinds of values need to be rediscovered today. Families forced to sell their farms and widespread corporate downsizing reflect a sad state of affairs. People are more important, too. Profits are necessary to stay in business, but loyalty to employees and a way of life count, too. Earning as much as possible is fine, but what we do with what we earn to love and serve others is more important.

Country values remind us that making a living is not as significant as living a life that embodies such merits as caring, understanding, cooperating, and forgiving. Our society judges a person for how he or she looks. We need to appreciate people for what they are, for intangibles like character and honesty and decency.

"Down On The Farm" reminds me of the old baseball story about the minor league team that played in a park without fences. In deep left field there was a pig pen. One of the players hit a long fly ball to left that landed right in the middle of the pen. One of the boars pounced on the baseball and ate it. At first, the umpire wanted to call it a ground-rule double, but then he changed his mind and called it an inside-the-pork homerun!

Confederate Railroad
"Elvis And Andy"

Some values bond people at a deeper level. The girl in Confederate Railroad's song and her future mother-in-law may not have agreed on much, but they did agree on liking Elvis. Ultimately in life, we need to find what we agree on rather than what we disagree on. We always have a choice in life to focus on the positive or the negative things. It is often a matter of perspective. As someone once said about the rose, "We can rejoice that thorns have roses, or be angry that roses have thorns." We can argue over different religions, different politics, different ways of looking at life, or we can rejoice that someone does at least have a religion, does care about politics, does look at life differently. Our differences add excitement and variety to life. We find that our differences often complete the picture, helping us to see things in ways we would never have seen on our own.

Many of our differences regarding our concept of God can be resolved by imagining God as an infinite diamond. Each person sees a different facet of the diamond; if we share our view of that beauty with others, everyone is enriched. However, if we insist that one particular way to envision God is the only way, then instead of more light in the world there is only more darkness. We always have the choice to add more understanding or more confusion to an issue, to add compassion or more criticism, to add healing or more hurt.

Polarizing people, dividing people, setting them against each other can be a way to get elected to a political office or win a war, but ultimately dividing people just adds to the hurt of life. Remember these often forgotten words of Jesus:

> Among the pagans the mighty make their importance felt. Those with power lord it over others. It cannot be that way with you. The one who would be first among you must serve the rest.

Jesus' words offer quite a contradiction to how much of our world works. That's why, as we live by our values in a world that devalues what is truly important, we need to know clearly what we want to be, and what we do not want to be.

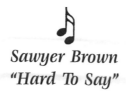

Sawyer Brown
"Hard To Say"

Many of our values go back to the country because we ultimately go back to the country. Before there were cities and suburban sprawl, there was only country. In the country, neighbor helps neighbor. In the city, people can live next door to one another and not know each other's name. In the country, there is great dependence on good weather for crops, and so people developed simple rituals and prayers to petition God for favorable conditions. Today, there is a sense of not needing God for food when the local grocery is just around the corner. As you can see, it's easy to move away from old values because of new situations. And yet, there is a price to be paid. Not to know or help our neighbor leads to the epidemic of loneliness experienced in our society. The absence of an immediate need to care about crops doesn't take away the reality that cities would perish rapidly without food. Rugged individualists are a rare breed today. Few of us make the clothes we wear or manufacture the car we drive. Few of us have our own business or grow our own food. Few of us write TV programs or direct movies. In short, we are all incredibly dependent on each other for almost everything, from eating to entertainment. But this dependence is lost on many.

"Hard To Say" highlights what it's like to live without values. Fate does not make a bad day. We make a day good or bad by what we do with it. Lies destroy relationships. If we cheat on our spouse, we end up only cheating ourselves. Yes, there are things that are hard to say, but we need to say them, like "I was wrong"; "I'm sorry"; "Will you forgive me?"

One of the most sacred values we have is to be a person

of our own word. To say what we mean, and to mean what we say. By being a person of strong moral conviction, a person of our word, we keep our promises to God and to each other. Being faithful to our word is always hard, but it is at the basis of our best values, in the country or in the city.

♪

Collin Raye
"Man Of My Word"

CHOOSING FREEDOM

Mary Chapin Carpenter
"I Take My Chances"

Freedom often involves taking chances. As Mary Chapin Carpenter sings, "I never learned nothing from playing it safe." Later on in the song she sings, "I don't cling to remorse or regret." A Jewish woman, explaining how she survived the atrocities and indignities of a concentration camp, once said, quite simply, "I do not hold on to hurtful memories." She used the image of standing in a fast flowing river. "I just let go, and let the currents of life take the pain from me."

Perhaps the first thing we need to do to be free is to live in the present moment. We lose our freedom if we carry regrets from the past, or live with anxiety about the future. When God revealed his name to Moses in the burning bush, God revealed his name as "I Am." A favorite meditation on God goes like this: "When you live in the past with its hurts and regrets, life is hard. My name is not 'I Was.' When you live in the future with its worries and anxieties, life is hard. My name is not 'I Will Be.' But when you live in the present, life is not hard. I am with you. My name is 'I Am.'" To be free is to live in the now, in the presence of God.

For some people, however, to be free means to live outside the law, to live by their own rules as renegades, rebels, and rogues.

Tracy Lawrence
"Renegades, Rebels & Rogues"

Some people, as rebels and rogues, just act out their pathologies and low self-esteem. An identity as a rebel may develop because one cannot fit in with mainstream life. Prisons are filled with people who were rebels, but many of these unfortunate souls were also people with learning disabilities and violent childhoods. They claimed their identity by succeeding in crime because they could not succeed in life.

The rebels and rogues Tracy Lawrence sings about, however, were not criminals, but people with a hard time living with structures and conventional life styles. Tracy described them in one line as having "eyes of fire and hearts of gold." Truly free people do not want to hurt others or themselves. Because they value their own lives and want to live it their own way, they also value the lives of others. We often speak of the "me" generation and condemn its inherent selfishness. Surely there is much selfishness, but the real distinction in people is between those who are hostile and those who are caring. The hostile person is someone with low self-esteem who thinks life is mean and others can't be trusted. Hostility is always a mask for low self-esteem. People with high self-esteem, who value themselves as children of God, are not hostile and love others precisely because they love themselves. Selfish people with low self-esteem put others down, and are harsh and critical. The person with true self-love is humble, caring, respectful of others. The truly free person is the person with genuine self-love.

Victor Frankl, who suffered as a prisoner in a Nazi death camp, wrote: "We who lived in concentration camps can remember those who walked through the huts comforting others, giving away their last piece of bread. They offer sufficient proof that everything can be taken away from a person but one thing: the last human freedom to choose one's attitude in any given set of circumstances." To be truly free is to love despite not being loved, to give without counting the cost, to choose to be loving even in a hateful environment.

Sadly, for many people living in our free society, the chains they wear are of their own making.

Lee Roy Parnell
"Take These Chains From My Heart"

No one has any control over us that we do not give to them. In "Take These Chains From My Heart," Lee Roy Parnell tells his girl to take away the chains, but he was really the one holding onto them. She had no power over him that he did not give to her. She may have looked attractive, or behaved seductively, or played on his feelings, but he still chose to cooperate, to be manipulated, to stay in her presence. As with most addictions, the object of our desire has no power that we do not bestow upon it ourselves. A bottle of whiskey just sits there. Drugs don't chase us down the street. Promiscuity is not forced upon people. All our thousands of addictions—addictions to work or play or sports or whatever—only have the power we give them. This does not mean that such addictions are easy to break. It just means that the answer is not in changing someone else. The answer lies in changing ourselves—saying no, letting go, refusing will power and trying a Higher Power.

As someone wisely said, "The problem with most addictions is not will power, but *won't* power." Self-discipline is an important part of self-love. In our culture, we are manipulated into thinking that the more we have the happier we will be. Advertisers manipulate us into becoming consumers. It should not surprise us, then, that a nation of consumers could easily become a nation of addicts. Material wealth does not guarantee personal happiness. Doing without, exercising self-discipline and valuing the spiritual over the material, frees us to make choices rather than be manipulated.

When I think of setting ourselves free, I think of the little girl who said to her mother, "Mommy, remember those teacups you always worried that I would break?" Her mother responded, "Yes, I remember." The little girl replied, "Well, Mom, you don't have anything to worry any more." The deed had been done, and the mother was suddenly worry-free.

We often create our own misery. We convince ourselves we need a drink, a drug, a set of dishes, a type of car, or anything else. As the great philosopher Socrates said thousands of years ago, "I love to walk through the marketplace and see the thousands of things I am happy without." Freedom begins within us, not within someone else.

Mark Chesnutt
"Woman, Sensuous Woman"

So many of our physical and emotional "chains" are self-imposed obstacles. The irony of our flawed choices is that they usually end in addiction, or at the very least leave us less free to choose wisely. For example, we are free to choose to get romantically involved with someone because of an initial physical attraction. We then risk choosing someone who may look good, but may not be good. All of our dissatisfaction with how we look has generally made Americans more self-hating, more critical, and less happy. Billions of dollars are spent on exercise and diets without any indication that people's habits have changed. Instead of expensive gizmos and fad diets, most of us might be better off simply consuming less fats, eating more fruits and vegetables each day, and taking a few brisk walks during the week.

Freedom means being free to say "yes" or "no," to make the right choices, to be our best selves not our worst selves. Someone once defined a truly selfish person not as someone who does what he or she wants to do, but rather someone who wants to make someone else do what he or she wants them to do. In other words, we are free to run our own lives, we are not free to run someone else's life, to harm them or not to care about them.

During World War II, Pastor Martin Niemoller wrote a great parable about how we are not free from caring about others. "In Germany," he wrote, "they came for the Communists and I didn't speak up because I wasn't a Communist. Then they came for the Jews, and I didn't speak up because I wasn't a Jew. Then they came for the trade unionists, and I didn't speak up because I wasn't a trade unionist. Then they came for the Catholics and I didn't speak up because I was a Protestant. Then they came for me—and by that time no one was left to speak up." While we are free to live our own lives, we are called to care about the lives of others. Independence grants us the freedom and ability to help others, not permission to hurt others.

♪

Martina McBride
"Independence Day"

We all have a right to declare our independence. We can free ourselves from childhood abuse, neglect, and fears. We can free ourselves from abusive marriages, not by harming our partner, but by getting away from our partner and protecting ourselves from further harm. We can free ourselves from self-hatred and self-punishment by developing healthier and happier images of ourselves through training, therapy, or pastoral counseling.

With freedom comes responsibility to follow a course of action. Just getting away from a situation or predicament is not enough. People who free themselves from one addiction often replace it with another. People who get out of abusive relationships often choose other abusive people as friends or spouses, especially if they have not learned to understand themselves and to respect themselves. We need to move away from the negative forces in our lives and move toward something better, something positive. We must choose to live by God's values, not our own.

Someone once defined a saint as someone who "willed one thing." They willed to be as much like God as possible. All of us are truly free when we will life, not death; when we will love, not hate; when we will compassion, not condemnation; when we will to live by the eternal values of God, not the passing fancies and pseudo-values of society. Let us will to be free, free from all that makes us less like God.

LIFE'S DISILLUSIONMENTS

Suzy Bogguss
"Hey Cinderella"

Of all of life's disillusionments, nothing hurts worse than our disappointments in love. Stories and movies end with the couple falling in love and living happily ever after. In reality, falling in love is the beginning of the story, not the end. Nothing is as good as first love, as falling in love, as being in love. Unfortunately, that doesn't last. As one young woman put it, "Before we got married, he told me he could not live without me. Now that we're married, he watches the football games!" He turned out not to be her Prince Charming. No doubt, she turned out not to be his Cinderella.

The glow of first love cannot last because when we first fall in love there are no negative associations tied to the other person. He or she is a blank slate onto which we project all of our own ideals. After living together for a while, negative characteristics and differences become apparent: he snores; she likes the house warmer than he does; he likes to watch sports; she wants to go shopping and so on. When we fall in love we think that this new, incredible person will meet all of our needs. When we get married we discover that this person has needs of his or her own.

Interestingly, even living with the other person before marriage does not really prepare us for what he or she will be like after marriage. Living together before marriage is really another form of intimate dating. Once we get married, all of our unconscious ideas and expectations of marriage kick in, and we discover that the person we thought we knew so well now seems like a complete stranger. Many people become angry or depressed, feeling like they were duped by the other person. Actually, it's just part of reality. In fact, the disillusionment that sometimes starts with marriage can get only worse as the years go on.

Mary Chapin Carpenter
"He Thinks He'll Keep Her"

Without a doubt, our worst disillusionment comes in the area of love. We get married because of all the joy and intimacy that wedlock can and should offer. We get divorced because of our expectations are often unrealistic. The song "He Thinks He'll Keep Her" never takes into consideration that she might not keep him! I recall the story of the man at his wife's fortieth birthday celebration. He said to her, "I think I'll trade you in for two twenty year olds." His wife replied sweetly, "Honey, you're not wired for 220." When we are upset with what someone else is not, it can be helpful to remember that they may be just as upset with what we are not. As someone wisely said about criticism, "When you point a finger at someone else, remember that three fingers are pointing back at you."

One of the greatest challenges in love and in life is to be faithful to our highest ideals rather than sink to our most basic instincts. In other words, we can divorce someone because they are not as sexy, or giving us as much sex as we want, or they gained weight, or whatever. We can get angry at someone for what they are not, and forget our ideals, promises, and good things in the marriage (such as the sex you do have; the children you had together; the history you have lived together). If we just listen to our selfishness, we can easily justify throwing someone else away. But that's not how God treated us when we botched up. That's not the model I want to give my children. If we listen to our ideals, we realize that's not what we vowed to do on our wedding day.

Cutting through all the complications of divorce, we can summarize marriage and divorce in two sentences: "We get married for many reasons, but we get divorced for only one. We're not friends any more." If friendship is rebuilt, then sex lives, commitments, and marriages can be rebuilt.

We can even be disillusioned with life itself. So many of us think we missed something, or are afraid we missed something, on life. Consequently, in the name of living, people do all kinds of destructive things. They throw away spouses, promises, and values. To grab a moment's pleasure, they throw away a life's commitment. For a drink, a drug, a sexual fling, life's real treasures are traded—treasures such as integrity, honesty, credibility. But, rather than beating ourselves with guilt, we should feel appropriate guilt and do what's possible to amend the damage. With God's help, we strive to do better in the future. As the saying goes: "There is no sinner without a future, and no saint without a past."

Living life to the fullest requires being the best person we can be, and not simply seeking the greatest amount of pleasure. Certainly there's nothing wrong with pleasure. We were created to enjoy life. But when we seek only pleasure, we too easily treat others as objects, to be used for our delight, a means to an ends, and then tossed away. The real problem with pornography and violent films is that people are packaged and depreciated for our amusement. We stop thinking of each other as being made in the image of God, and instead view each other as mere objects.

A baseball manager coaching a championship little league game offered a great lesson in integrity. A runner raced around third and would have scored easily with the winning run, but the coach ordered him back to third base. In explaining what he did after the game, the coach told the player, "You missed third base!" The player replied, "But the umpire didn't see it." The coach said, "But I did." That run cost the team the championship. The team lost the game, but learned a valuable lesson about living a principled life.

When the great Michelangelo was painting the ceiling of the Sistine Chapel, someone asked him why he spent so much time and energy on places that no one could see. He answered, "Because God sees it." If we have traded away our integrity in life, we better get it back.

George Strait
"I'd Like To Have That One Back"

We can regret our choices. People who gave up on spouses often learn too late how good that person was. We can't always get that person back. Kids' games embrace a wonderful notion of "do-over" whenever controversy or an undesired result arises. Real life does not come with such an option. The best we can do after a regrettable choice is learn how to live life better. Here are nine suggestions for getting all you can out of life:

First, pray. Ask God for the courage and desire to

do his will. Bring to God your concerns and the needs of others. Learn to enjoy the presence of God.

Second, be gentle with yourself. Shun self-pity, as well as inappropriate shame or guilt.

Third, concentrate on the present and the future. Learn from the past, but don't dwell on it.

Fourth, cultivate qualities like compassion, honesty, respect.

Fifth, find ways to practice just being kind.

Sixth, use your energy to solve problems, not to run from them or fight your circumstances.

Seventh, learn to have fun. Play a game, tell jokes, take a walk, read a humorous book, sing a song.

Eighth, learn from others. Praise and imitate what's good. Learn from what isn't good.

Ninth, believe in something bigger than yourself, like God.

Then, as St. Paul said, "You will lead a life worthy of the Lord and pleasing to him in every way. You will multiply good works of every sort and grow in the knowledge of God."

John Michael Montgomery
"I Swear"

MOTIVATION

Wynonna
"Rock Bottom"

Adversity can crush some people, and bring out the best in others. What makes the difference? Years ago, Dr. Ann Kaiser Stears wrote a book called *The Triumphant Survivors* in which she documented how some people don't just survive tragedy, but seem to come back stronger for having survived. One of the people she interviewed was Edgar Alvarez, who survived eight-and-a-half years in a North Vietnamese prison. Alvarez fought the trauma by taking life one minute at a time. "I can endure this pain one more minute," he said, "this torture one more minute, this cell one more minute." One secret, then, is to break life down into manageable chunks.

A little pamphlet called *Self-Discovery Notebook* by Lisa Englehardt is another handy tool to surviving tough times. Here are just three ways she suggests that we discover new strength by self-discovery:

1. Are there ways you find yourself behaving that aren't really the way you want to be? Explore how

you learned the behavior, perhaps as a way to survive. Know and feel the difference between then and now. You don't have to continue to behave in ways that hurt you or others.

2. When you feel trapped, try drawing or writing about some creative options. Just knowing you have alternatives will help.

3. What beliefs did you form in childhood that you know were distorted? For instance, you may have assumed you were a bad person because of how someone treated you. Reflect on what is really true.

To look at it another way, people who are motivated by adversity rather than crushed by adversity learn to value themselves, to learn from their past, and to believe every situation can be managed. Just saying the words "I'll handle it" can have great results in dissolving fear and fortifying courage to face misery. "I'll handle it. I'll walk away a winner."

Kathy Mattea
"Walking Away A Winner"

Whatever actually motivates us to turn our lives around, the turning point always starts with self-respect—believing we deserve better than we are getting. Women may "act out" sexually because of adolescent pressures and needs, because of low self-esteem, because they were sexually abused early in life, or are involved in alcohol or other drugs. But deep down every woman wants a sexual relationship only if it is monogamous, only if her partner respects her, is faithful to her, and treats her with care and understanding. Men may "act out" sexually for many of the same reasons. Our often male-dominated culture erroneously gives men permission to behave differently than women. American culture is permeated with "machismo," an exaggerated sense of masculinity that demands men to be thick-skinned and frowns upon displays of feminine traits. But, just like women, men long for something deeper than pleasure. The key to motivating a man is to make him feel appreciated. The key to motivating a woman is to make her feel respected.

Three suggestions that help build self-respect are taken from a pamphlet by Linus Murdy entitled *Keep Life Simple*:

> First, learn the art of saying no. When you exclude something, you inevitably include something else more fully.
>
> Second, do not pretend to be anything you are not. That way you can always be consistent and truly free.
>
> Third, learn to value the spiritual things over material things. They last longer, cost less, bring more.

Pam Tillis
"Spilled Perfume"

Sometimes misery can be a strange ally. If we're miserable long enough, we might just get tired of it, and make some changes. At some point, we get tired of our self-defeating behavior, tired of hating ourselves in the morning, tired of looking for pleasure and finding only sadness. Many women talk about a new celibacy today, a decision to stop having sex with various partners and to stop putting their happiness in the hands of someone else. When we are motivated to reclaim our life, then we are motivated to do something better with our life. Motivation starts with a decision to make ourselves and our lives better. All change starts with the decision to do something.

Change often begins as it did for Pam Tillis, as sung in her tune "Spilled Perfume." Change begins when we are able to forgive ourselves. Mercy is so important. I saw a little card on Divine Mercy Sunday that noted the ABC's of mercy: A - Ask God for mercy; B - Be merciful to yourself; C - Complete trust in God. Or, as I rewrote it, "Show your trust in God by asking God for mercy. Be merciful to others. Care enough about others to be merciful to them." Too often in life we focus on ourselves individually and forget that we are all connected. The key to self-love and self-respect is the desire to be of service to others.

Unlike the girl in "Spilled Perfume," who got hurt and manipulated because she thought the guy could give her the moon, when we respect ourselves and are motivated by love, then we find ourselves choosing others who are good for us, and motivating them to rope the moon.

John Michael Montgomery
"Rope The Moon"

If love is the main source of life's disillusionments, it also possesses a miraculous motivational effect. As John Michael Montgomery sings, "I can't lose with her next to me." People who are determined to make themselves better will also help others to be better. Having a baby motivates many people to change. Here are some helpful thoughts from a reflection called "To A Baby": "You are the one we held onto so tightly. You are the link with our past, a reason for tomorrow. You darkened our hair, quickened our steps, squared our shoulders, restored our vision, and gave us a sense of humor, that security, maturity, and durability can't provide."

Mostly, however, people are motivated to change by having a healthy relationship with themselves, other people, and God. How do we build self-worth? A passage from *Keeping Up Your Spirits Therapy* by Linda Allison-Lewis provides some hints:

1. Forgive someone you're angry at. You'll feel light as a feather.
2. Forgive yourself in an instant. God does.
3. Don't despair. A broken heart can mend if we give God all the pieces.
4. Never compare yourself with another. You were formed with great precision.
5. Accept others without condition. It's the very essence of love.

Finally, having rebuilt our self-worth and perception of others, we want to rebuild our relationship with God. Keith McClellan, OSB, in a booklet called *Prayer-Therapy*, offers sound advice:

1. Prayer is yearning for one's true home. Follow its lead.
2. Let your prayer be short. Love needs few words.
3. Pray where you are. God is everywhere.
4. When your praying becomes dry and routine, keep at it. Parched earth welcomes the rain.
5. Bring your anger to prayer. Hot metal can be molded.
6. When you sin and continue to fail, pray anyway. God keeps on loving you.

Finally, a last thought from Linus Murdy: "Know that your true home is in the Holy Presence. It's that simple." In the presence of the Holy, we find an amazing love.

John Berry
"Your Love Amazes Me"

FORGIVENESS

Mary Chapin Carpenter
"He Thinks He'll Keep Her"

Decisions made in anger are rarely good ones. In "He Thinks He'll Keep Her," the woman played the dutiful wife for years, secretly being angry all the while, until finally deciding to leave the man. Unfortunately, as the song reveals, she ended up miserable, or more miserable, as a result of her decision. The big secret to a good life involves forgiveness, not revenge, which simply multiplies wounds. As Martin Luther King once said, "Revenge makes us even, but forgiveness makes us better."

I'm not talking about shallow forgiveness that enables someone to continue to hurt or abuse us. True forgiveness confronts the hurtful behavior, refusing to accept it, and then, once the behavior has stopped, enables us to forgive the offender. Victims cannot be silent. Not speaking up for ourselves keeps us in the victim's role. Then, as the woman did in Mary Chapin Carpenter's song, we just further victimize ourselves. If you're in a poor relationship, get counseling together. If your partner refuses, get counseling for yourself. Improve your self-worth, and, if the relationship won't improve, at least you are not dooming yourself to an unhappy life after it ends.

Unfortunately, rather than respond to a difficulty, we often react. "Response" means we take time to plan, to grow, to make good choices. "React" means we operate at the level of impulse. We want to get even. Revenge will make us even, it just won't make things better!

Trisha Yearwood
"Better Your Heart Than Mine"

How do we turn taking revenge on a partner into taking better care of ourselves? In "Better Your Heart Than Mine," Trisha Yearwood mentions some healthy ways to emerge from a breakup. She stopped the hurt, refused to allow the man back into her life, learned boundaries and set limits. These actions are healthy. What's unhealthy is that she seems to hold onto her anger, enjoying the fact that it was better that his heart broke than hers.

The irony of life is that we can protect ourselves without hurting someone else, and, in fact, the more we rejoice in someone else's pain, the more we hold onto our hurt and pain. Respecting ourselves does not mean we have to disrespect others. Jesus had a marvelous way of not letting people control him, of moving on to new villages when others wanted him to stay in their village, but he never was nasty about it. He just said he had to move on. His ultimate act of letting go of anger was when Jesus was able to pray for those who tortured and killed him: "Father, forgive them. They do not know what they do."

I'm reminded of the true story of a young seminarian, a twenty-two-year-old man studying for the ministry, who was killed on Christmas Eve. Apparently he had a premonition of his death, because he left the following note behind: "I see myself killed on the road leading to my village. If this happens, I say to my mother and my sister, do not be sad, we will be together again. Forgive those who have killed me. May my blood be mingled with that of all the victims who have fallen, from all sides and all religious confessions, be offered as the price of peace, of love, and of understanding which have disappeared from this country, and from the entire world. Pray. Pray. Pray. And love your enemies."

In every situation in life, we always have a choice to be kind or cruel. Too often we make the cruel choice.

Linda Davis
"Company Time"

Life in the work world is often needlessly tough. The girl in Linda Davis' "Company Time" is able to rise above the put-downs. But we don't have to be so mean. When I give workshops in private industry, I try to help people build their own sense of self-worth so that they can build up other people. When you wonder how to treat someone else, ask yourself how you would treat a son or daughter, or grandson or granddaughter. How would you want others to treat someone you loved? Then treat others that way, or go and do likewise. Efficiency at work is increased by kindness, not cruelty. Obviously, you have to set limits. There are people who would take advantage of kind people. As some Filipino women, who came to this country to work, once said, "People in this culture mistake meekness for weakness." It takes strength to be just and fair and respectful. The coward is cruel and insensitive.

There's a little reflection I like about a man's search in life for the good. It was written by John O'Reilly, and reads as follows:

"What is the real good?"
 I asked in musing mood.
"Order," said the law court;
 "Knowledge," said the school.
"Truth," said the wise man;
 "Pleasure," said the fool.
"Love," said the maiden;
 "Beauty," said the page.
"Freedom," said the dreamer;
 "Home," said the sage.
"Fame," said the soldier;
 "Calmness," said the seer.
But spoke my heart so sadly,
 "The answer is not here."
Then within my bosom
 Softly this I heard:
"Each heart holds the secret-
 'Kindness' is the word."

Our wisdom does tell us that kindness is the way to live. Unfortunately, that's not always what we choose.

Sammy Kershaw
"I Can't Reach Her Anymore"

Sometimes we have to accept that we make mistakes, unlike the man in "I Can't Reach Her Anymore," who could not reach his partner because he had first chosen to walk out on her. Rather than blame her for staying out of his reach, he needed to reflect on what he did to make her avoid him, and admit that he was wrong.

Rather than constantly hurting each other, what are some things we need to be aware of that help us to appreciate each other? Here are nine concepts for validating others:

1. All people are unique and must be treated as individuals.
2. All people are valuable, no matter how disappointing their behavior.
3. There is a reason behind the behavior of people.
4. Behavior is not merely a function of changes in the brain, but reflects a combination of physical, social, psychological and spiritual changes that take place over the lifespan.
5. People cannot be forced to change. Behaviors can be changed only if the person wants to change them.
6. People must be accepted non-judgmentally.
7. Particular life tasks are associated with each stage of life. Failure to complete a task at the appropriate stage of life may lead to psychological problems.
8. Painful feelings that are expressed, acknowledged and validated by a trusted listener will diminish. Painful feelings that are ignored or suppressed will gain strength.
9. Empathy, identifying with another person's feelings, can build trust, reduce anxiety and restore dignity.

These are just some ways that can end the crying, and begin the healing.

McBride & The Ride
"No More Cryin'"

Change must occur within ourselves. As long as we stay angry at someone else, as long as we blame someone else, as long as we stay focused on someone else, then we give away our power to control our own lives, and the power to heal. Someone has said that "riches means living with a lot of things, and power means not needing to have a lot of things." I suggest choosing power, the power to control your life, the power not to let anyone else hurt you, the power to not let anyone else's opinion or judgment control your life.

When we blame or complain, nothing changes. I think of the story of the three little bears. The Papa bear said, "Somebody's eaten all my porridge." The Baby bear said, "Somebody's eaten all my porridge." The Mama bear said, "What are you two complaining about. I haven't made the porridge yet!" A friend once said sarcastically that the only exercise some people get is running other people down, jumping to conclusions, and dodging responsibility.

It's easier to wear slippers than to carpet the world, or in other words, we only get better by changing ourselves, not changing others. When we change our way of thinking, our attitudes toward life, our self-defeating patterns, then the world miraculously changes.

Count your blessings, name them one by one, and you'll notice that your blessings outweigh your curses. There is more good in life than bad; more people who love us than hate us; more people who wish us well than people who wish us ill. We give power to the negative by thinking about the negative. We give power to ourselves by thinking about all that is good and right with life. Let's live not with thoughts of getting even that keep us hurting. Let's live with thoughts of thanks that help us grow and heal.

Emmylou Harris
"Thanks To You"

FROM INNOCENCE TO CYNICISM

Diamond Rio
"Sawmill Road"

The process of growing up and growing older can be disillusioning. On Sawmill Road, life was simple. But Vietnam was not simple for Billy Joe, nor were relationships simple for Mary Beth. As the song tells us, "innocence went out of style."

Life seems simple when we're young, and we discover how complicated it is as we grow up. An anti-war protester put it this way: "When I was in my twenties, life seemed black and white. As I grew older, I realized that there's a lot of gray." Life is not simple for any of us, and no one has all the answers. (Not even priests!) I preach to others, but I have struggles in my own life. Just like anyone, I need encouragement and support. There's a little poem by Leslie Pinckney Hill entitled "The Teacher" that gives me hope:

Lord, who am I to teach the way
To little children day by day,
So prone myself to go astray.

I teach them knowledge, but I know
How faint they flicker and how low
The candles of my knowledge glow.

I teach them power to will and do,
But only now to learn anew
My own great weakness thru and thru.

I teach them love for all mankind
And all God's creatures, but I find
My love comes lagging far behind.

Lord, if their guide I still must be,
Oh, let the little children see
The teacher leaning hard on thee.

There's a great wisdom in that poem, isn't there? Disillusionment with life and with ourselves can lead to cynicism, or it can lead us to God. We have choices. We can fall in the water, and we can also learn to swim.

John Anderson
"I Fell In The Water"

Many people become cynical about love. Two lines in John Anderson's song say it all. The first is "I thought you could do no wrong." In our naive, innocent state, we idealize the person we are in love with. The second is "You're nowhere near to what you appear to me." Reality sets in, often too late, revealing that the qualities we saw were qualities in our own minds, not in the other person. We call that "projection"—seeing in someone else what is really in us.

People often get hurt when they innocently project desirable character traits onto others. If someone is straightforward, honest, and sincere, it's easy to project those qualities onto someone who is neither honest, nor sincere, nor straightforward. And when reality strikes, we embrace a cynical attitude about love.

Several responses help us from becoming cynical in love. One is to recognize a mistake. If we are married to an abusive person, we need to refuse to accept the abuse, to seek counseling, and, if necessary, to get away from a person who will not change. This helps us become self protective, not cynical. A second response is that when we idealize someone else, we may be seeing qualities that are there, that love can bring out, but which takes time. Sometimes a lover sees things no one else sees. This turns disillusionment to commitment. The third response is to realize that maybe we were blinded by our desire, and need to mature. In other words, this person may not have been what we thought he was, but maybe he is still a good person. If we're disillusioned because we didn't get what we wanted, maybe we need to mature and love someone else as he or she is!

Sometimes, however, despite wisdom and maturity and our best efforts to love, a relationship just won't work. Like a bad movie, there comes a time for an ending. "I finally saw a movie with a happy ending," someone once astutely commented. "Everyone was happy it ended!" Sometimes we just have to admit that a particular person is not for us.

Confederate Railroad
"She Never Cried"

We all come from God's hand, but we don't all live and

act like God's children. The truth of life is that we all are re-flections of the image and likeness of God. However, as a result of abuse and neglect and trauma, and personality disorders, we can lose our sense of self-worth, and live with a distorted view of life. People who are miserable to others have first been miserable in their own lives. People who are happy want to share their happiness. People who have been hurt, seem to want to spread the pain. That's not the way life has to be, but too often that is the way life is.

Ironically, those who will hurt us the most, especially in relationships, are often the smoothest talkers, best dressers, and best looking. People who do not have themselves to-gether on the inside invariably seek to compensate by look-ing good on the outside. There's an eternal wisdom to the old saying that "you can't judge a book by its cover." The bible reminds us that "people see the appearance, but God sees the heart."

The head and the heart reflect two styles of communi-cation. To speak from the heart is to speak honestly, with-out guile, without holding back. To speak from the head is often to be manipulative, to say what someone else wants to hear, to dominate rather than communicate. Sometimes we think we're getting a message from the heart, only to be sur-prised that it's really the head speaking. The surprise end-ing to this poem helps separate the "head" from the "heart":

> There are three words...the sweetest words
> In all of human speech,
> More sweet than all the songs of birds,
> On pages poets preach.
> This life may be a vale of tears,
> A sad and dreary thing.
> Three words and troubles disappear
> And birds begin to sing.
> Three words and all the roses bloom,

The sun begins to shine.
Three words will dissipate the gloom
  And water turns to wine.
Three words will cheer the saddest days
  "I love you"...wrong, by heck!
It is another sweeter phrase,
  ENCLOSED FIND CHECK

Tracy Lawrence
"If The Good Die Young"

While innocence may die young, the good do not always die young, which reminds me of the story of the meanest man in town who finally died. At his funeral, the preacher asked if anyone wanted to offer any words about the man's life. There was a long, embarrassed silence, as everyone sat quietly with nothing good to say about the mean man. Finally, an elderly gentleman, one of the kindest people in town, stood up and said, "Well, sometimes old Jake weren't as mean as he was most of the time."

Innocence is not determined by age, but by behavior. We do not have to grow bitter and cynical as we grow older. Cynicism, ultimately, can be unmasked as an excuse for underachieving in life. The person who is cynical, who blames his or her problems on others, who always bemoans his or her bad luck, ultimately is someone who spends more time complaining than working.

I remember one summer job I had back when I was in college. There was a co-worker who used to spend hours setting up ingenious warning devices to alert him to the supervisor's approach. Ironically, if he had spent the time working that he spent setting warning devices, he would have had a far easier day. When he got fired, he was cynical and bitter. He blamed the boss instead of looking at his own performance.

Life is tough for all of us. We all get discouraged and depressed. We all experience injustices. But instead of letting life's tough times make us bitter, we can let them make us better. If we have been treated unfairly, it can become an opportunity, not to get revenge, but to treat others fairly and justly, since we know how it feels to be treated unfairly. If we feel discouraged or depressed, it can help us be more compassionate toward other discouraged people. Instead of putting them down, we can help build them up.

Here's a little poem, I don't recall the writer, that can help us get perspective when we feel tempted to become cynical:

> If times are hard and you feel blue,
>   Think of others worrying too.
> Just because your trials are many,
>   Don't think the rest of us haven't any.
>
> Life is made up of smiles and tears,
>   Joys and sorrows mixed with fears;
> And though to us it seems one-sided,
>   Trouble is pretty well divided
>
> If we could look in every heart,
>   We'll find that each one has it's part.
> And those who travel fortune's road,
>   Sometimes carry the biggest load.

The poem helps us realize that no one has an easy life, not even those who seem to have it made in the shade. The cure for cynicism is to develop compassion. All of us have enough pain in life. No one needs any more hurts or put-downs. We all need more support and care. All of us are searching for love.

Boy Howdy
"She'd Give Anything"

Many people take the trip from innocence to cynicism, but we do not have to make the journey. To be sure, all of us get disillusioned with life. We can get discouraged with the pain of life. But we don't have to become cynics. Good friends can help us. Humor can help us keep perspective. God certainly must have a sense of humor, having first created us, and then deciding to save us.

The love we so often search for is a love we already have. The kingdom is within us. The love of God has been poured into our hearts by the Holy Spirit who was given to us, St. Paul reminded us. In short, we can become cynical about those who do not love us, or we can become excited about those we can love. There are people in nursing homes, in hospitals, at soup kitchens, in shelters, who would love to have someone love them. We can turn in on ourselves and feel sorry for ourselves, and blame the world for not making us happy, or we can get involved in making someone else happy, and then we will find the love we have searched for. The paradox of life is true. We get only by giving. We find life only by dying. If we hang on to our hurt, we will stay hurting. If we help someone else, we find our hurt mattering less.

Cynicism is another form of self-hatred. But we were not created to hate; we were created to love. Art Fetig wrote the so-called "Self-Esteem Creed." When we learn to believe that God believes in us, it becomes a lot easier to have faith in ourselves. The creed unravels as follows:

> God made me. I was no accident.
> I was in God's plan.
> And He doesn't make junk, ever.
> I was born to be
> A successful human being.
> I am somebody special, unique,
> Definitely one of a kind.
> And I love me.
> That is essential so that
> I might love you, too.
> I have talents, potentials, yes,
> There is greatness in me, and
> If I harness that specialness,
> Then I will write my name
> With my deeds...
> I was born in God's image
> And likeness,
> And I will strive to do
> God's will.

Life is not about turning to cynicism, but about turning to God. And when we return to God, we return to our innocence. We realize that life is not about being cynical, about what we do not have, but enjoying what we do have - the sun and trees and nature and friends and love. The kingdom is within us and all around us. We stop being cynical when we open our eyes and see the miracle of life around us and the miracle of life that we are. We are created by God, redeemed by God, and at the journey's end, we return to God. Hey, maybe we do have it made in the shade!

John Anderson
"I've Got It Made"

DEFEATING DEPRESSION

Clint Black
"State Of Mind"

When we understand how our state of mind affects our lives, we realize how important it is to hold a positive attitude toward life. As the great psychologist William James said, "The greatest discovery of this age is that by changing our thinking we can change our lives."

Imagine what a difference it is to wake up and say: "Oh, no, another day. I have to get up. I hate this!" Contrast that to waking up and thanking God for a new day of life, looking forward to the surprises God has in store for you, and realizing no other day will be exactly like this one. There's a true story a man told about his seventh birthday. He remembered what a happy day it was, what nice presents he received, what wonderful people were around him. But he said as he went to bed that night, for the first time in his life he grasped his mortality. He knew he would never have this day to live over. He knew he would not live forever.

Facing our mortality can lead some people to ask "What's it all about if I'm going to die?" while others exclaim "Wow, I've only got a limited amount of time on this planet, so I better make each day count!"

Our state of mind determines almost everything. A song can cheer us in the midst of depression. Another song can depress us if we associate it with a lost love or a lost path. The key is to begin to realize that while we can't always control what happens to us, we can control our attitude toward what happens to us. Worrying and fretting set us up to expect the worst. Prayer and confidence set us up to believe that nothing is going to happen today, tomorrow or any day, that God and I together can't handle! Our mind can look at a cemetery and see a rose garden. Or we can look at a rose garden and turn it into a cemetery. It's a matter of perspective.

Boy Howdy
"She'd Give Anything"

Desperation, like anger, rarely paves the way to good choices. "She'd do anything to fall in love" usually means that she will get hurt, used and abused, and still not find love. It's not in our best interests to suddenly decide that we absolutely need a romantic partner. As a baseball manager once said, "Any time you want to make a trade in the worst way, you usually will." In other words, in romance or in sports, if we are desperate to get someone, the odds are good that someone will take advantage of us. Desperation makes us "ripe for the pickin'."

Why frustrate yourself trying to find someone to love us, when it makes more sense to learn to love ourselves? Yes, life can be lonely, but marriage can be lonely, too. Being single may mean that we do not have one particular person in our lives, but it does not mean that we cannot cultivate other relationships—with brothers, sisters, cousins, friends, etc. If we miss having children, there are plenty of kids longing to share love with someone else, and lots of parents only too happy to have you borrow their kids to take to a game, or a movie, or the circus, and so on. In other words, people spend all their energies on developing a romantic relationship, and ignore other equally vital and rich relationships. If we decide we won't be happy unless we are married, then we can succeed in making ourselves unhappy. If we decide we can enjoy life even if we are not married, then we can do things that make us happy. Life is what we make of it!

In life we have to make choices about who we are, and how we will live. I love this little poem:

Within my earthly temple, there's a crowd.
There's one of us that's humble and one that's proud.
There's one that's brokenhearted for his sins.
And one who, unrepentant, sits and grins.
There's one who loves his neighbor as himself.
And one who cares for naught but fame and self.
From such corroding care I would be free,
If once I could determine which is me.

We alone decide if it's rejoicing time or if it's crying time. Choices are ours to make.

Lorrie Morgan
"Crying Time"

Our attitude affects our mood. True, we do have to honor our feelings. After a loss we do have to grieve, to feel our anger, to experience the depression, to go through the bargaining and denial, and finally arrive at acceptance. There is no timeline on grief. One person may recover in a year; someone else may take five years. However, a wise person put it so well when she said, "Grieving is a process. Recovery is a decision."

Some people never seem to get over a loss. They define their life by the loss. Other people grieve, feel the loss, and then move on. They do not forget the person or the incident, but they realize that they do not honor the lost person by dishonoring themselves. In honor of a lost child, or lost spouse, they resolve to live each day to the fullest. Rather than stay stuck in self pity, they use the pain of the loss to get involved in groups that help other people who have lost children, or have lost spouses. We do have choices in life. We can choose to be bitter or better. We can let our pain make us more sensitive to the pain of others, and become more caring and more compassionate. Or we can let the pain of life make us angry and bitter and depressed. We always have choices. Life is not just what happens to us, but how we choose to respond to what happens to us.

When I think of feelings of anger, I think of the story of the lion roaring in the jungle and asking, "Who is the King of the Beasts?" The zebra bowed and said, "You, O mighty lion." The antelope bowed and said, "You are the king of the beasts, O mighty lion." The elephant, however, wrapped his trunk around the lion, picked him up and swung him around, and threw the lion against a tree, knocking him out! When the lion awoke he looked up at the elephant and said, "Look, just because you didn't know the answer doesn't mean you had to get mad!"

Toby Keith
"A Little Less Talk And A Lot More Action"

How can we go about doing things to make life better? If we just sit and wait for life to get better, the odds are good that nothing will change. If we go out and risk we might just make things better. Going out to a bar or night club may not be a real good investment of our time if we are looking for a lasting relationship. However, doing things does make a difference. They have done studies indicating that we cannot be physically active and depressed at the same time. If you feel depressed, take a brisk walk. Within an hour you will find your mood changing. Sometimes, when we are stuck in depression, we cannot think our way into feeling good, so we have to act in a way that makes us feel good. We can change our lives by changing our attitude and we can change our attitude by changing our behavior.

I'm reminded of a brief reflection by Joseph R. Sizoo, who wrote the following passage:

> Life is a race. Don't whimper if the track is rough and the goal is distant. One day you shall reach it. Life is a voyage. Don't complain if the storms batter the hull or the winds tatter to shreds the sail. One day you shall come to your haven. Life is growth. Don't find fault if the seed lies smothered and submerged in the dark earth before it blooms and blossoms. One day you shall have your harvest. Life is a pilgrimage. Don't falter on the road through self pity because stones cut your feet and leave your blood on the trail. One day you will come to Immanuel's land. The God who, through the boundless sky, guides the flight of the sparrow, who builds the blind bird's nest, will see to it that in his good time you shall arrive.

Our attitude determines our life. We can waste our life bemoaning what is not, or we can make a decision to really live until we die.

Clay Walker
"Live Until I Die"

Much of life is affected by our state of mind. Every accomplishment, every achievement, every thing we see around us, once started as an idea in someone's mind. A sex therapist once commented that our largest sexual organ is our brain! Our sexual thoughts, our fantasies, our decision on how to behave starts in our brains. Unlike animals who survive on instinct, we survive on our wits.

To live until we die means to really live each moment of life. We do not waste time on regret, or beat ourselves up for mistakes. We do not surrender to addictions, nor do we yield to popular opinion. As a great philosopher once said, "Every great idea started out as a heresy or blasphemy." When Jesus spoke of God as his "Father," he was accused of blasphemy. When Galileo said the sun was the center of the solar system, he was accused of heresy. We need to live in such a way that what we leave in our wills will help someone else to make something of their life.

When we think of how our attitudes change our lives, we realize that our attitude toward life changes life. On this theme, Raymond B. Fosdick wrote a very good reflection:

> The only life worth living is the adventurous life. Of such a life the dominant characteristic is that it is unafraid. Like Columbus, it dares not only to assert a belief but to live it in the face of contrary opinion. It does not adapt either its pace or its objectives to the pace and objectives of its neighbor. A life worth living

thinks its own thoughts. It reads its own books. It develops its own hobbies. It is governed by its own conscience. The herd may graze where it pleases or stampede where it pleases, but he who lives the adventurous life will remain unafraid when he finds himself alone.

That would be a great statement to leave in our wills, wouldn't it? It might be supplemented by the words of Helen Keller, who said, "I long to accomplish a great and noble task, but it is my chief duty to accomplish humble tasks as though they were great and noble. The world is moved along, not by the mighty shoves of its heroes, but also by the aggregate of the tiny pushes of each honest worker."

♪

Mark Chesnutt
"The Will"

EMOTIONAL HEALING

Diamond Rio
"Sawmill Road"

I mentioned before how life on the Sawmill Road re-
flected a simpler, more innocent time. Part of life's hurt,
however, is a loss of innocence. After a trip to Saigon for one
song's characters, and a fourth husband for another, there
was the realization that life was not going to stay innocent.
I'm reminded of an interview with Jane Fonda when she
was asked about her anti-war work protesting the Vietnam
War. She basically responded that when you are young, life
is black and white; as you grow older, you realize how complicated life can be. But with growth, chronological and spiritual growth, comes knowledge. As we learn from our own
mistakes, we learn that compassion toward others is wise.
As we learn from our own disillusionments, we learn that
helping others when they go through a divorce, or when
they get hurt, when they lose a job is wise. As we face how
complicated life is, we learn that keeping a simple value system in a complicated world is wise.

The reason that the ten commandments and the law of
love and the Golden Rule never go out of style is that they

help us keep a simple perspective of right and wrong despite the life's complexities. As we learn the harsh lesson that we are not always in control of life, we learn how important it is to let God be in control of our lives. General Dwight D. Eisenhower—the supreme commander of the allied forces during World War II, and later President—was a very practical person. He once said very simply, "This is what I found out about religion: it gives you courage to make the decisions you must make in a crisis and the confidence to leave the results to a higher power. Only by trust in God can a man carrying responsibility find repose." If we trust in God, we begin to heal from hurt. If we place our trust entirely in someone else, we may just get more hurt!

Rick Trevino
"Just Enough Rope"

Emotional abuse is a downward spiral in which people often get trapped. One way to continue to get hurt is to allow others to jerk us around. When you get a chance, listen to "Just Enough Rope." It sounds sort of cute, until you realize how manipulated the main character was, manipulated by love. We often hear of women being abused, but men can be abused, also, if they let it happen. We are, as Carl Jung said, mixtures of male and female energies, amalgamation of masculine and feminine characteristics. By nature and nurture, one side often predominates. Wholeness and holiness come from integrating our two sides: the masculine side of competing, doing, fixing and our feminine side of caring, respecting, and loving. The man in "Just Enough Rope" allows himself to be used. He does not use his masculine energy to set boundaries. He does not demand the respect that he deserved. Many women get abused when they keep giving respect and care, but do not receive respect and care in return.

The simple formula is to ask for what you need. If you don't sense the other person cares about your needs, this is a signal that this person does not respect you. We are our worst enemies when we do not respect ourselves, and do not demand respect from others.

When I think of being worst enemies, I recall the story of two buddies at work. One said to his friend, "Man, you sure are hard at work." His friend replied, "No, I'm just fooling the boss. I'm carrying the same cartons in and out all day!" There's a great message in that little parable. We usually hurt ourselves when we try to hurt someone else. In life, we are usually at our best when we do our best, and expect the best in return. We get hurt when we don't respect ourselves, and we get hurt if we hang around people who don't seem to respect anyone or anything.

Confederate Railroad
"She Never Cried"

We can set ourselves up for a lot of hurt when we hang around hurtful people. Think of images from the Confederate Railroad song: she didn't stand up for the National Anthem; she didn't cry for Old Yeller; eventually, she was rude to his mother. People that are disrespectful of others have often been treated disrespectfully themselves. However, they need to seek counseling, to get help to heal from old wounds, not take out their hurts on others. "He who gossips to you will gossip about you," so goes the old saying. We might also add that he who is disrespectful of others will eventually disrespect you. Love is blind, but try to keep an open eye. Too often, when we are in the throes of romance, we might not see (or want to see) defects in our partner. Marriage can be a rude, and late, wake up call. Love can be blind. Best to get a vision test before the vows are blessed.

I'll never forget a wedding I presided over years ago. The couple printed a program, and right in the middle appeared the misprint "The couple will now exchange vowels." A sort of matrimonial "Wheel of Fortune," I suppose. Well, in life we can avoid some heartache if we "change our spelling," so to speak. However, we set ourselves up for more heartache if we expect someone else to change.

Mark Collie
"Something's Gonna Change Her Mind"

Life requires thought. We need to choose to be our best selves, to hang around good people not destructive people, to respect ourselves and expect respect from others. We also need to know that we can change no one except ourselves. "Something's Gonna Change Her Mind" sums up a lot of pain for a lot of people. There are people who have put their lives on hold waiting for someone to come back, waiting for someone to change his or her mind, waiting for someone to be different. Why do we do that?

Well, there are surely many reasons. One may be that we don't really have good self esteem. We don't think anyone else could or would want us. A second reason why we may hang on to a dead relationship is that we made vows and we want to keep those vows. While this is a noble ideal, reality says that we can only stay with someone who wants to stay with us. Ten years after a divorce, if we are still waiting for this other person to come home, it may just prove that holding on to an ideal does not mean we can hold on to a person. A third reason why we may hold on long after a relationship is dead is based on false pride. We may not be able to deal with our feelings of having failed. Again, here it is important to emphasize that, while one relationship did not work, we are not failures ourselves. We all make mistakes. We need to forgive ourselves, forgive the other person and move on. Whatever the reason for holding on, I need to realize that I can control my behavior, but I can't control someone else's. At some point we have to stop torturing ourselves with what cannot be and let go and let God takeover.

When I think of behavior that makes no sense, I think of the story of the man riding a bus. Every time the bus stopped the man on the seat next to him took a French horn and blew it. Finally the first man asked him, "Why do you blow that horn every time the bus stops?" The second man replied, "Oh, it keeps elephants from charging the bus." "But there isn't an elephant within a thousand miles," the first man protested. The second man replied, "It works, doesn't it?"

Next to waiting for someone else to change, another way we hurt ourselves is by waiting for someone else to get hurt. Hoping someone else will get hurt may satisfy our anger, but it will never make us happy.

Patty Loveless
"You Will"

Often we get hurt when we give control of our lives to someone else. We are doomed to unhappiness if we decide to wait for someone else to change, to wait for someone else to get hurt. We cannot be happy by giving control of our lives to someone else.

We become happy by taking responsibility for our lives and behavior and giving control of our lives only to God. Taking responsibility for our lives means deciding to make good choices. One choice is to slow down. Orin L. Crain's wonderful prayer offers the following petition:

> Slow me down, Lord. Ease the pounding of my heart by the quieting of my mind. Steady my hurried pace with a vision of the eternal reach of time. Give me, in the midst of confusion, the calmness of the everlasting hills. Break the tension of my nerves with the soothing memory of quiet streams. Teach me the art of taking one minute vacations—to look at a flower; to chat with an old friend or make a new one; to pet a dog or watch a spider build a nest; to smile at a child or read a good book. Remind me each day, Lord, that the race is not always to the swift; that there is more to life than increasing its speed. Let me look toward the towering oak and know that it grew great and strong because it grew slowly and well.

We take back responsibility for our lives by slowing down to discover what is important in life. Then we surrender to God by developing certain attitudes that help us be aware of God. Penning a little formula for life, Henry van Dyke wrote the following:

> Be glad of life because it gives you the chance to love and to work and to play and to look up at the stars. Be satisfied with your possessions but not content with yourself until you have made the best of them. Despise nothing in the world except falsehood and meanness. Fear nothing except cowardice. Be governed by what you admire, not what you hate.

Covet nothing that is your neighbor's except his kindness of heart and gentleness of manners. Think seldom of your enemies. Think often of your friends. Think every day of God. And spend as much time as you can with your God each day.

In life we all hurt and get hurt. We may not always be the best fathers, but we all have a Father in heaven who wants the best for us. In life, a father loves to be called daddy. When we grow close to God our Father, then God becomes our Abba, the one we do call Our Daddy!

♪

Doug Supernaw
"I Don't Call Him Daddy"

DON'T MISS THE (LIFE) BOAT

John Anderson
"I Wish I Could Have Been There"

Sometimes, people easily miss the essence of life. People can literally miss the life boat. It's so easy for us men to become workaholics, to make our job our life. We do that at the risk of missing the life of those we love—our wives and children, our parents and brothers and sisters. It doesn't have to be that way. I think of two examples of people who kept their priorities straight.

One case is a man in his late forties, who is director of an important state job. He rarely misses a day of work, works hard while he is at work, but never takes work home. "If I can't get it done at work, it's not going to get done that day." In assuming that posture, he has missed some opportunities for advancement, but none he regrets. However, he has four children, and never misses a game, never misses one of his children's performances in dance or debate, never plans anything that does not include his children. To me, he's a hero of the real world.

Emerson once said that there are some people too great to be famous. I'm convinced that the really famous are never the truly great! Yes, there are good people who are famous. Yet, while the world looks at Mother Teresa with deserved admiration, I think of the nun who goes with her to get her awards, the nun whom no one knows, the one too great to be famous. I see performers who get fame and wealth, but I often think of the truly great technician behind the scenes who never gets noticed. We see presidents of companies and countries who are in the public eye, but only because countless other people are working behind the scenes. The truly great people are not famous.

A second example of keeping one's priorities in line stars a young woman in her thirties, earning over $80,000 a year, who asked for a leave of absence. Her boss told her that she was on the "fast track," sure to be considered for a job at the top. But she responded, "I want time to be with people who matter to me." Parents don't live forever. Children don't stay young forever. We may think we're too busy to watch games, or go to graduations, or attend school plays or performances. But work will go on, and these may never come again.

Kim Hill
"Janie's Gone Fishin'"

As in life, so in love. We may have gone after someone else who looked better, and lost the person who was better. The man in Kim Hill's song learned too late that the woman was the one he really loved. By the time he realized it, she had "gone fishin'." "She refused to be a slave to misery, when there's plenty of fish in the sea." She learned self-respect. Amazingly, when we set high standards, we net quality people. I remember an eighty-year-old lady talking about a time when her sister was on a date. The boy got fresh with her, so she slapped him. Another guy, hearing about it, said, "That's the kind of girl I want." He wanted a girl who respected herself, because this is the type of person he wanted to mother his children, and to love him. People who respect themselves will respect others.

In our society we are actually conditioned to ignore what is important. We are trained through advertising and fashion and even the media to look a certain way, talk a certain way, walk a certain way, even think a certain way. When we chase after what is unimportant, like looks or clothes, we miss what is really important—the ability to care, love, give, and respect others.

Often in life, we not only miss life and love, but we even miss something as important as God. As John Henry Newman once wrote, "I sought to hear the voice of God and climbed the highest steeple. But God declared 'Go down again, I dwell among the people.'" In our humility we see God in other people. In our pride we just hurt ourselves, and hurt each other.

Travis Tritt
"Foolish Pride"

Pride causes us to miss a lot, too. False pride, the pride that is a deadly sin, is that part of us that is fearful, that is afraid to forgive or ask forgiveness, the part of us that hides behind a mask of hostility. How many marriages have ended because someone was too proud to ask for help, to go to a counselor with a real sincere desire to work on a marriage? How many relationships have ended because someone refused to say "I'm sorry"? How many arguments have been fought, feelings hurt and trust damaged, because someone was too proud to say "You were right"? Pride is the mask of an insecure person who mistakes rigidity for strength.

In our pride, instead of talking to a counselor, or asking help from a priest, minister, rabbi or other religious person, too many turn to drugs. Instead of reaching for a phone, they reach for a bottle. People who say "I'll solve it on my own" usually end up solving nothing and injuring others.

For many people suffering from depression, alcohol is their preferred therapy. Here's a little reflection by Richard Blummer about alcohol:

> We drink for joy, and become miserable. We drink for sociability and become argumentative. We drink for sophistication and become obnoxious. We drink to help us sleep and awake exhausted. We drink for exhilaration and end up depressed. We drink to gain confidence and become afraid. We drink to make conversation flow and become incoherent. We drink to diminish our problems and see them multiply.

A powerful reflection, and only too true. In our faith we reach for God. In our fear, we reach for a bottle, and wonder why we cry.

Daron Norwood
"Cowboys Don't Cry"

If we miss the life boat, we are left with tears, depression, and disappointment. Someone described hell as waking up in eternity, and realizing we had spent our lives pursuing an unfaithful lover! In other words, instead of pursuing God, the one who loves us unconditionally—the one who forgives and calls us to life here and to eternal life hereafter—we pursue something less. Instead of pursuing the living God, we stalk a strange god of money or power or fame. Instead of loving one special person, we chose to give in to our lust for many people. Instead of living in the joy of knowing God's love for us, we chose the "highs" of our addictions. How sad to wake up at the end of life and realize that objects of our lust don't love us back. How sad to realize too late that once we're buried, no one will care about the kind of car we drove or how much money we made.

I think of a little plaque that read: "A hundred years from now, no one will care what kind of car you drove, house you lived in, or salary you earned. But if you made yourself important in the life of a child, that will live forever." Imagine waking up in eternity only to realize that the bottle cleaved to didn't really love you in return; that the sports team you spent so many seasons following didn't really matter; that the drugs you sought so desperately were a poor substitute for the God you forgot to seek.

Ultimately, only God satisfies, because only God can meet the infinite longings of the human heart. Our hearts are restless until they rest in God. God goes on forever. Everything else in life will stop on a dime.

Little Texas
"Stop On A Dime"

Our consumer-oriented society conditions us to be buyers and spenders. Every program you watch or listen to is filled with commercials which are designed to make you feel bad about yourself, so you will buy something to make yourself feel better. So we buy and eat and drink and drug. And all we discover is that it is never enough. Nothing outside us will ever satisfy us. The kingdom of God is within you, Jesus reminded us. God is within us. When we realize God is within us at this moment, we develop a new awareness of ourselves, new respect for others, new care for the world. To find what is important in life, we need to make the inner journey, the journey into our own souls and psyches and spirits.

A good image for exploring our inner worlds is the image of the cycle of the seasons—spring, summer, autumn, and winter. From a spring perspective, is there something in your life that you need to birth, to give life to? From a summer perspective, is there something in your life that's bearing fruit—the result of hard work, study, new goals? From an autumn perspective, is there something in your life that you need to let go of, as a tree lets go of its leaves? From a winter perspective, is there something in your life that has died, or feels frozen? The seasons help us to look at our inner life in order to discover what is important in us and to us. We need to listen to our inner selves.

Ultimately, to find what is important we need to discover God. A selection from the writings of Leo Cardinal Suenens describes how faith promotes positive attitudes. He wrote:

> God is here, near us. Unforeseeable and loving. I am a man of hope, not for human reasons nor from any natural optimism, but because I believe the Holy Spirit is at work in the Church and in the world, even where His name remains unheard. I am an optimist because I believe the Holy Spirit is the Spirit of creation. To those who welcome him, he gives each day fresh liberty and renewed joy and trust. The long history of the Church is filled with the wonders of the

Holy Spirit. Think only of the prophets and saints who, in times of darkness, have discovered a spring of grace and shed beams of light on our path. Who would dare to say that the love and imagination of God is exhausted? To hope is a duty, not a luxury. To hope is not to dream, but to turn dreams into reality. Happy are those who dream dreams and are ready to pay the price to make them come true.

If we have found God, we will not miss anything that is important in life. The most important things are the most basic things, and every believer in Jesus knows these three things: our sins are forgiven, our lives have meaning, and we are going to live forever.

♪

Hal Ketchum
"Drive On"

LOSS

Keeping Faith While Coping With Grief

SAYING GOODBYE

Blackhawk
"Goodbye Says It All"

The meaning of "goodbye" has come a long way from its original intent. "God be with ye" was a blessing that God would be with the person departing. In "Goodbye Says It All," however, the woman's goodbye scrawled in lipstick on the wall probably intended something other than a blessing. "No chance of redemption, no further exemption," Blackhawk sings. Hardly the stuff of God, who came into this world for redemption, and always finds a way to forgive us.

When coping with the initial shock of goodbye, whether it's a loved-one moving away or the death of a spouse, one of the first things we need to do is find God. Stop the world, step back from the pain, and get away from all the noise. We need to get away from our cares and fears and be alone with God. At a time of loss we feel so abandoned by God, when in reality God is so close that we can't see him! A little poem by Louise Imogen Guiney captures this reality:

The little cares that fretted me
  I lost them yesterday

Among the fields above the sea,
  Among the winds at play.

The foolish fears of what might happen,
  I cast them all away
Among the clover scented grass
  Among the new-mown hay.

Among the husking of the corn,
  Where drowsy poppies nod.
Where ill thoughts die and good are born,
  Out in the fields with God.

We heal from goodbye when we make goodbye what it really means—being with God. When we can be with God, we may yet learn how not to disagree with each other.

Billy Dean
"We Just Disagree"

Often, disagreements end in separation. "Seems you lost your feeling for me," Billy Dean sings. In reality, separation is the last option, not the first. Disagreements don't mean we're bad for each other, just different from each other. If we can talk it out, we don't have to fight it out. If you can't talk it out, go to a counselor. The most expensive marriage counselor is still cheaper than a divorce. Problems in a marriage are just part of being human. Resolving problems and being closer as a result of talking and compromise, these are the things that border on divinity.

Again, the key here is the "God" in goodbye. If God is not the third party in our marriages, the odds are good that the marriages won't last. We humans, on our own, are acutely aware of what we are not. God, however, reminds us of all we can be. A wonderful little parable by Lyman Abbott about an acorn illustrates the potential we all possess:

> I pluck an acorn and hold it to my ear, and this is what it says to me: "By and by the birds will come and nest in me. By and by I will furnish shade for the cattle. By and by I will provide warmth for the home. By and by I will be shelter from the storm to those who have gone under the roof. By and by I will be the strong ribs of a great vessel, and the tempest will beat against me in vain, while I carry people across the Atlantic." "O foolish little acorn, will you be all this?" I ask. And the acorn answers, "Yes, God and I."

When we trust God in the by and by, we may never have to say goodbye!

Steve Wariner
"Driving And Crying"

Loss forces us through the stages of grief: depression, denial, anger, bargaining and finally, acceptance. It's not easy burying our dreams. It's as hard as burying a loved one, which it really is. We lay to rest our dreams and hopes. As a poet once penned, "No sadder words than these, it might have been."

How do we protect ourselves against goodbye? How can we get to really know someone before we marry them? There's a light-hearted parable about the young man going to the wise man asking how he could find out the secret faults of his intended wife. The wise man responded, "It is quite easy. Gather all her closest friends and tell them how wonderful you think she is. They will tell you all her faults."

The only problem with that advice is that in the stage of falling in love, we don't want to hear about someone's faults! In reality, the best way to insure a happy marriage is not just to find the right person, but to be the right person. In other words, if we can make ourselves the best people we can be, we just might find less to complain about in our partner. Failing that, we need to learn from our mistakes, to mourn our losses, and to rebuild our sense of self esteem. A divorce means a relationship has failed. A divorce does not mean we are failures! We bury a past but not our future. I don't think we ever really get over a major loss, but we do adapt to it. In the healing process, be gentle with yourself. Feelings have a way of ambushing us. Just when we think something is over, suddenly we hear a song on the radio, and we're right back into our hurt and tears.

Reba McEntire
"They Asked About You"

People do not get over losing a loved one, rather we adapt to the loss. We need to take time to grieve, to perhaps join a bereavement group, to seek counseling. We need to grieve at our own pace, and on our own schedule. There is no time limit on grief. Don't pretend to feel better if you do not. Don't let anyone force you to speed up your grief.

While grief is a process, recovery is a decision. We have to make a decision to go on. We do not honor the memory of a deceased loved one by living the rest of our lives in grief, but we honor them by living fully in their memory. If someone has divorced or abandoned us, we need to believe that we are worth living for. Our life has not ended even though a relationship has. We are not less whole because we are less a couple.

In life we are what we and God make of ourselves, not what someone else thinks of us. Helen Hayes, the actress, wrote the following words of wisdom, which I think are profound:

> My mother drew a distinction between achievement and success. She said that achievement is the knowledge that you have studied and worked hard and done the best that is in you. Success is being praised by others, and that's nice, but not as important or satisfying. Always aim for achievement and forget about success.

In life, we are meant to be the best selves we can be. And if we're lucky, we might just find another self to spend life with. For some that's another person. For all of us the real love of our life must be the Lord of Life.

Neal McCoy
"No Doubt About It"

DEALING WITH LITTLE DEATHS

Randy Travis
"Before You Kill Us All"

As sure as love and life go together, death and separation seem to go together as well. When the girl in Randy Travis' song left, more than the guy was dying, so was the dog, the cat, the plants, and on and on. When I think of a cat having used up eight of its nine lives, I think of the story of the little girl's kitty that died, and her mother tried to console her daughter, and said, "Honey, your kitty is now in heaven with God!" The little girl responded indignantly, "Mommy, what would God want with a dead cat?"

Ultimately, God does not want our death but our life. God wants us to have the fullness of life, so that's why God sets slaves free, and raises up the dead. That's also why we call God Love. Love always gives life. Lack of love seems to hasten death. Years ago, the book *The Broken Heart: The Medical Consequences of Loneliness* documented how separated, widowed, and divorced people suffered more illnesses and died younger than married people. Needless to say, as an "unwed Father," so to speak, I wasn't too pleased with the conclusions. Ultimately, though, even if a marriage or relationship should fail, the secret to a long and healthy life involves cultivating good friendships.

In the song above, however, while Randy Travis blamed the girl for killing the relationship; in reality, he was the one who allowed things to die. Right or wrong, she was going on with her life. He could, unfortunately, choose to die in a depression, neglecting himself and the other things in his life, or he could have chosen life. Even if others have wronged us, we do ourselves no favor living in depression, or spending our time blaming others. Often late in life we discover one of life's greatest pieces of wisdom and that is we only frustrate ourselves trying to control someone else. Ultimately, we cannot make someone else love us. We can't even make someone else call us!

Reba McEntire
"Why Haven't I Heard From You"

Unfortunately, some people die from lack of love long before we die from lack of breath. The secret to rediscovering life is not to blame someone else for not calling or not wanting to be with us, but to look at ourselves and see how we can be better people. As a wise person put it, marriage is based not just on finding the right person, but on being the right person.

Sadly, in our society we emphasize sex so much that we forget that love is so much more. To put things in perspective, allow me to quote a few paragraphs from an article by Lauren Griffin:

> The whole world has passed you by. Everyone is doing it. Everyone is enjoying it. They have drama and romance and make love all night. Sometimes all

day.

You, on the other hand, have endless baskets of laundry, a husband who snores, and children who think you're a taxi service. If you don't do something, you'll be left behind.

Sound familiar? It should; it is our culture's most popular propaganda and many of us have welcomed it with open arms and eager libidos.

Sex has become the barometer defining what constitutes a vital relationship. If the excitement of the early days can't be induced back in a five-, ten-, or fifteen-year marriage, then the conclusion is clear. The magic is gone and the only way to bring it back is with someone else. Parents find themselves divorced and dating just as their teenagers are preparing for the junior prom.

The primacy of sex has thwarted the natural phases of an individual's life, arresting our development at the (adolescent) stage when getting a hand up or down of someone else's clothing was the greatest of all achievements. At the time, maybe it was. Although the sexual intimacy of young adulthood is very compelling, we have to remember that it isn't an end, but a beginning. If we allow ourselves to grow, this passion will lead us into a much deeper and wonderful mystery."

Sex in itself can never match the redemptive power of friendship and commitment in a marriage. This commitment learns to haul through the hard roads. Children test and strain this commitment, but they transform this love into something much greater than it ever would have been.

Later in life, this love continues with the forgiving and tender attention of a grandparent. We need to value these things. If we are unable to appreciate the natural rhythms of the life cycle, with sex in perspective, we ultimately will divest our lives of all mystery.

Powerful thoughts! We need someone to teach us how to live and love, and how to say goodbye.

Patty Loveless
"How Can I Help You Say Goodbye"

Previously, I talked about goodbyes. It has been said that "goodbye is a little death; death is a big goodbye." If we understood the basic meaning of goodbye, however, that it means "God be with you (ye)", then we might not be so afraid of death or goodbye.

In the cycle of life, death is a part of life. In our neurotic American culture, where we try to deny death, death is the destruction of life. If we can mature to the point where we see death as just the next stage, we might transform ourselves forever. As one down-home philosopher put it, your body is like your car—it is the way you get around for a number of years, but it is not you. Just as the time comes to trade the car in, to let it be recycled, there comes a time to let go of the body. This does not mean that the body is not good, that it is not to be valued as a temple of the Holy Spirit, it simply is to be recognized as one way of being, not the only way of being. As Christians, we believe that we will receive our bodies back again, in a glorified state, in the resurrection of the dead. Immediately after death, our spirits become part of God's spirit. Life is changed, not ended. When the body of our earthly dwelling lies in death, we gain an everlasting dwelling place in heaven.

The reason why it's so important to put sex, and all other bodily pleasures in perspective, is not that they are bad, but that there is so much more to each other than our bodies. Love is eternal, because love is able to value what is eternal in us. Our physical appearances will change. Regardless of diet, exercise, or anything else, a sixty year old will not look like a twenty year old. If we confuse the person with the package, we doom ourselves to a frantic effort to stay young. Supposedly even Brezhnev and other old leaders of the Soviet Union were obsessed in their later years with finding pills and drugs to keep them alive, to reverse the aging process. I suppose if you're an atheist, death is a terrible thing, the end of it all. If you're a believer, death can be an exciting stage, an entrance into a new and marvelous existence, something so wonderful that eye has not seen and ear has not heard.

Certainly there will always be sadness in the loss of physical life, or the loss of a relationship, because we mourn what we lose. Change is difficult because we tend to want to hold on to what we have. As someone wisely put it, "The last time most of us want any change is when it happens to be our diaper." But change is easier if we know there is life after death and new hope after an old relationship. Yes, it is a shame to lose something that once was good. But we cry less if we believe that there might be something better in our future.

The Mavericks
"What A Crying Shame"

It is a shame when something good dies. We need to take time to cry, to mourn, to honor our feelings. As a wise person said: "Grief is a process. Recovery is a decision." In other words, we grieve differently. Some people may complete in a few months what it takes other people years to mourn. Don't allow anyone else to force your feelings. However, at some point, we have to decide to live again. That decision turns our life around, it begins the process of life after the death of a relationship.

How do we go on after someone has left us, especially if the parting has been hurtful? Here are five suggestions taken from a booklet called *Forgiveness Therapy* by David Schell:

> First, you have the right to feel sad, betrayed, angry, resentful, when you've been injured. Understand, accept, and express your feelings. Pushing feelings below the surface only means they will erupt in another place, at another time.
>
> Second, confront those who have hurt you. Tell them how you feel. When that's impossible, or when that could harm you or someone else, speak to them in your imagination, or write it out.
>
> Third, justice may right the wrongs, but forgiveness heals the hurts. Seek forgiveness beyond justice.
>
> Fourth, sometimes people hurt you because, like you, they are learning and growing. Forgive their incompleteness, their humanness.
>
> Fifth, and finally, to refuse to forgive is to continue to hurt yourself. Victimized once, your lack of forgiveness keeps you stuck as a victim. Identify instead, claim the identity, of one who forgives.

Holding on to our hurt only keeps us miserable. We do not deserve to live as miserable people. God created us for the fullness of life. And ultimately, perhaps that is the secret message of our hurts and pains and disappointments and deaths. Our incompleteness yearns for completeness. Our hearts are restless until they rest in God. We yearn for that eternal intimacy with God, that place where life never ends, that place where hearts aren't broken and no one ever says goodbye.

♪

Brother Phelps
"Eagle Over Angel"

LETTING HOPE REPAIR DESPAIR

Merle Haggard
"In My Next Life"

Some people have lost hope, at least in this life. He hoped that in his next life, he would be a hero to his wife, someone who could be proud of him. I think that song points out how important a woman's love and appreciation and support are to a man. Many women complain that men do not say "I love you" enough, but they sometimes forget that men's jobs are often their way of saying "I love you." They want to be able to provide for their wives.

A lifestyle is not nearly as important to most women as a life with someone who is devoted to her. He might have asked her how she felt about him, rather than presumed she was not proud of him. I recall the tragic story of the man at his wife's deathbed. He said to her, "You were always the most important person in the world to me." His wife replied sadly, "Why did you wait so long to tell me?" We all need to hear words of thanks and appreciation and praise.

One antidote to despair is to sit down today and make a list of fifty things you are grateful for! You can list everything from good health to food to a beautiful day to a car that did start today! Then you might repeat this exercise each day. You see, when we are tempted to despair, we are reflecting on the things that did not go right, things we do not have, disappointments in life. Reflecting on what we do have, what we are grateful for, begins to build a kind of emotional bank account. We develop an attitude of gratitude, and like a miracle, it begins to change how we look at life. Happiness is not somewhere else. Happiness may be as close as our own backyard.

Joe Diffie
"In My Own Backyard"

If we are to find hope in the midst of despair, we must realize that happiness is where we already are, not somewhere else. He discovered too late that happiness was in the little things—children playing, laughter, time with his wife and children. As creatures of our culture, we get addicted to thrills. We think each moment of life must be exciting. But joy in life doesn't come from thrills but from being fully awake, being fully alive, in the present moment. Too often we live either in the past with regrets and guilt, or in the future with worries and anxieties, and we miss the present.

I heard a powerful story of a man living on a farm in South Africa when diamonds were discovered there. He put his farm up for sale, and spent his life in search of diamonds. He found none, and eventually died, despondent and despairing. One day, the man who bought his farm was walking down by the stream that ran through the farm, and saw some shining rocks in the stream. He had discovered some of the largest diamonds ever found. The first man had sold his farm to look for diamonds somewhere else, when there was a whole field of diamonds right in his own back-yard.

There are diamonds all around us—people to be loved, things to be done, services we can provide for others that will help them and support us. If you are wondering what to do with your life, ask yourself a simple question: "What service can I provide for others?" If you have skills and abilities and talents that will help others, you have discovered the diamonds in your life, and if you use your abilities to help others, someone will pay you for them. The question is not "Who will give me a job?" but rather "How can I be of service to others?" The irony of life is that when we focus on helping others, we always also help ourselves.

There are diamonds where we are, whether we live in the center of the city, or on the outskirts of town!

Sawyer Brown
"Outskirts Of Town"

We have to plant a dream if we want to water it with hope. As a wise person once said, "Beware of what you set your heart on in life, for you will surely get it." It does not matter where we are, the city or suburbs, in the skyscrapers or the mountain foothills, we all need a dream. And while life may put limits on us, we don't have to put limits on our dreams.

How can we make our dreams come true right where we are in life? Cheryl Jarvis wrote a wonderful article entitled "The Case For Staying Home With The Kids." She had two children and dropped out of the employment world twice— once full-time for five years, and once part-time for another five years. However, rather than give up her dreams because of children, she discovered greater dreams. Ms. Jarvis writes:

> In fact, it was after I stayed home with my children that I landed my dream jobs. Something must have been going on during those years. I'll tell you what was going on. I had time to think, something I rarely did when I was juggling a full-time job and a small child. Time to think about what I wanted to do with my life. During those years I learned to live with insecurity and fear.
>
> When it came to pursuing the jobs I wanted, I risked going into the unknown. When you don't have a conventional job to lose, taking risks is easier. And I landed jobs on the strength of my ideas. Ideas come from making connections, and you make connections, not just from observing and reading but from listening. It was during the years at home that I really learned to listen. Isn't that what parenting is all about?
>
> Women who drop out no longer conform to society's view of achievement, so we create new definitions of our own. I've done a lot in my life that some people might envy, but when I think of my achievements, I don't think of things, I think of my sons. I am in awe of them, not just of their accomplishments but of their natures, generous, compassionate, adventurous and independent. It is through raising them that I became an adult, through raising them that I forgave my parents, through raising them that I discovered what life is really about.
>
> With creative thinking and an upbeat attitude, we can always find ways to use our talents, we can always acquire new skills. But there are no second acts when it comes to raising kids. When they are little,

we think they are gifts, but when they grow up we realize they were only a loan.

The cost of dropping out of the work force depends on the value you give your memories. I've found that the memories that sustain me during life's bleaker moments are not of the jobs that are no more. The memories that sustain me are those of my sons. I stayed home with them less than the time I was in elementary school, but the memories of those years are mine forever. I think I got a great return on my investment.

Cheryl Jarvis was obviously not addicted to a dollar!

Doug Stone
"Addicted To A Dollar"

Hope comes from believing in ourselves and believing in God. The two are related. If we do not believe in God, we will often make a god of something else, money, power, prestige, our possessions. We will show people the stuff we have rather than the stuff we are made of. If we believe in God we know we are made of the stuff of divinity, in the image and likeness of God. We have hope because we know that, if God is for us, who can be against us.

We get addicted to a dollar only if we have lost our sense of being worth so much more. A very insightful person put it so wisely. She said, "Every recovery program, every twelve step program, has reference to a higher power. If we call on a higher power in recovery, why don't we call on a higher power in prevention?" To put it another way, if we know we need God to restore our wholeness, why not call on God to keep us whole? Religion is not for weak people. Religion is for those who want the best for themselves, for their spouse, for their children, and families and neighbors and co-workers. Wouldn't you like to be around someone who wanted you to experience joy and happiness daily, who wanted you to experience faith, hope and love every day of life, and who wanted you to live forever?

Too often we think of religious people as people who want to control us. Some people will use religion that way. They confuse God's will with their will. But truly religious people are people who want us to be free, free of addictions, free of low self esteem, free of self-defeating behaviors. Belief in God can prevent us from hitting rock bottom. I'll never forget a true story a man told me of laying in bed one night for three hours, with a gun pointed at his head in one hand, and a crucifix in the other. He kept looking at the crucifix, a cross with the body of Jesus on it, and then he would look back at the gun. He had to choose between self destruction and salvation. Fortunately, he chose salvation. He chose God.

Belief in God can prevent us from hitting rock bottom, and belief in God can help us when we do hit rock bottom.

Wynonna
"Rock Bottom"

Fortunately, we are never without hope. The kingdom of God is within each of us. The presence of God is within each of us. Sometimes we have eyes and do not see the presence of God. That's the only real blindness. There are people who may be physically blind but who are well aware of God's presence. They can truly see!

All of us need to rediscover our own dignity and special-ness. Wynonna sings about being able to turn life around once she had hit rock bottom. When life puts us down, we need to let God pick us up. We need to rediscover our po-tential, our ideals, our qualities. The following reflection is aimed specifically at building up the image of women:

> The universe was yet incomplete, and so on the sixth day God created her—WOMAN! And God said to her, "I shall give you:
> A heart full of compassion
> A spirit free to fly with the birds
> A vessel to carry life into the world
> Wisdom to know great truths
> Courage to rise out of oppression
> Strength to move mountains
> Gentleness to kiss the earth
> Passion to set the world on fire
> Vision to respect the earth that bore you
> A playful nature to dance with the children
> Laughter to fill the valleys
> Tears to wash the pain away
> Hands for laboring and loving
> Intuition to know the unknown
> Desire to be that which you were created to be."
> And God said to her, "Woman, I have created you in my Image and Likeness and YOU ARE GOOD!"

A beautiful reflection written by Susan Marie. We dis-cover how amazing we are, when we discover how amazing God's love for us really is.

John Berry
"Your Love Amazes Me"

WORRY AND FAITH

Lee Roy Parnell
"I'm Holding My Own"

Thinking about worry, we all say things similar to what Lee Roy Parnell sings in "I'm Holding My Own," don't worry bout me. Sometimes that's a false bravado. We pretend to be feeling better than we are. Sometimes "don't worry" is an angry statement, as it was in that song. Don't worry about me because I'm taking better care of me than you did. I'm better off without you.

Ultimately, we can say not to worry, but it's really hard to do it—to *not* worry! Sometimes women will use the word worry as a way of expressing love and concern. "Oh, I'm so worried about my son or daughter." In the sense of caring about someone else, worry can be a sign of love.

Most often, though, worry is a form of self punishment. We worry to the point that we don't feel secure with life. We don't trust ourselves. We don't trust others. We even may have a hard time trusting God. Erik Erikson, in his stages of psychological development, says that trust versus mistrust is the first stage of development toward a healthy ego. Obviously, many of us never navigate that first stage.

Someone has wisely said that worry is trying to face life without God at our side. Worry presumes we're going at it alone. Faith presumes God is going with us through life, and even if we fail or make mistakes, God will be there to forgive and pick us up again.

Some studies show the futility of worry. One study indicated that 40% of what we worry about is past, which we can do nothing about. Another 30% of our worries are about things that never happen. Another 20% of our worries are about things that do happen, but which we have no control over. Roughly 10% then of all our worries are about things that we can do something about. Not very productive, is it? Sometimes I think we worry, much the way people used to beat drums. We worry as a way of warding off bad things. Unfortunately, worry or not, bad things can still happen.

Alan Jackson
"(Who Says) You Can't Have It All?"

We mourn what we do not have or make the best of what we do have. "Who says we can't have lots of misery?" seems to be the theme of Alan Jackson's song. Yet, while there was depression and sadness in his lonely "shrine to the blues," there was some wisdom. He did have four walls, a ceiling, a bed and pillow. As absurd as that may sound, an awful lot of the world has less. One cure for worry then is gratitude. Rather than worry about what we do not have, we can choose to be grateful for what we do have. We do have choices in life. We can choose to worry, or not. We can choose to be happy, or not. We can choose to love, or not. Worry gives the control to someone else to make us miserable. Being content and peaceful is taking back control of our own lives, deciding we deserve to be happy rather that miserable. Ironically, many, if not most, of us don't really allow ourselves to feel too happy. For some reason, we seem to limit our joy and our happiness. Worry is certainly one way to spoil our happiness.

Someone once offered the following little reflection on why we have nothing to worry about:

> There are only two things in life to worry about, whether you have good health or bad health. If you have good health, there's nothing to worry about. If you have bad health, there's only two things to worry about, whether you'll live or die. If you live, there's nothing to worry about. If you die, there's only two things to worry about, whether you'll go to heaven or hell. If you go to heaven, there's nothing to worry about, and if you go to hell, you'll be spending so much time shaking hands with all your friends, that there will be no time to worry.

Well, that meditation may help some, but I would worry less standing outside the fire!

Garth Brooks
"Standing Outside The Fire"

One way people attempt to avoid worry is by trying to avoid life. By standing outside the fire, by standing apart from passion and relationships and commitments, and involving ourselves in worthwhile projects, we hope to avoid hurt and failure and disappointment. In a sense, deciding not to live does take the worry out of life, but what's the purpose of life? The purpose of life is to know, love and serve others as we attempt to know, love and serve God. And this involves risk. Attempting to know God involves risk. If we get to know the living God, the living God may ask something of us we do not want to do. It's risky loving someone else. They may not love us back. However, they also might love us back. It's risky serving someone else. We might get used. Or, we might make a difference for good in the world. In other words, taking the risks is better than worrying about why we should not take the risks.

On the lighter side, when I think of worry, I think of the story of the man worrying about his health, so he went to the doctor for a check-up. After his examination, the doctor called the wife into his office. The doctor told her, "Mrs. Jones, I'm afraid your husband might die. "What can I do to help him?" the wife asked. The doctor replied, "Well, your husband is in such fragile health, the only way he'll live is if he has no frustrations at all in his life. So you must meet his every need. If he wants sex, give him sex. If he wants to watch football all the time, let him watch football. If he wants to go out with the guys, let him go out with the guys. Whatever he wants to do, let him do it. You must have no thought for your own feelings, but you must indulge your husband's every whim and fancy."

As she and her husband were driving home, the husband asked his wife: "What did the doctor say?" His wife replied, "He said you were going to die!"

Well, it takes a cool customer not to worry. Sometimes we have to live the way we drive-on cruise control!

Dennis Robbins
"Mona Lisa On Cruise Control"

There are people who seem to always be cool, always be in control, always calm. It's important to realize that such a calm exterior can be a mask. In reality, everyone has anxious moments. The key is not to let our anxiety control us, and not to make our anxiety worse by worrying.

What exactly is worry? Worry is taking the clouds of tomorrow and putting them over the sun today. Worry is trying to cross bridges before we get to them, something no one can do. Worry is looking at the problem, not at God, the solution to the problem. Worry is living expecting the worst. Worry is self punishment, stealing the joy of today by living in fear of tomorrow. Worry is an addiction. We think if we worry we will do better. Excitement may help us, but worry usually just tenses us up and makes us under-perform.

So worry can take many self-destructive forms. What helps relieve worry? Belief in God helps. It won't change a habit overnight, but at least we know we're not alone. Letting go of our worrisome thoughts helps too. Sometimes we may need to just get rid of our troublesome thoughts, if we have to drag them out of our lives kicking and screaming. Helping someone else helps worry too. Rather than worrying about what might happen tomorrow, help someone else today, and make things better for someone else today. There's a story of a nun who got a flat tire in a dangerous section of town. A big, tough looking guy stopped and changed her tire for her. When he finished, the nun said to him, "Oh, you're the answer to my prayers." The tough guy replied, "Lady, it's been a long time since I've been the answer to anybody's prayers!"

Helping someone else helps us by taking the focus off of our problems and letting us see what we can do for others. Just imagine, if all of us looked out for each other, what a great world this would be!

Another good cure for worry is not to do things that will

cause us more worry!

Tanya Tucker
"We Don't Have To Do This"

A way to avoid worry is to avoid behavior we have to worry about. Someone has wisely said that the secret to a happy life is either a good conscience or a bad memory. I suggest the good conscience.

We do have choices in life. We can choose to worry, or to use our time constructively. We can fret about the future, or we can live the present to the fullest and trust the future to God. As Jesus said, "Sufficient for the day are the worries thereof."

My final cure for worry is laughter. Laughter helps us to put life in perspective. The following joke is one of my current favorites:

Sadly, former President Bush eventually died and went to heaven. As St. Peter showed him around heaven, he saw Moses and introduced President Bush to him. Moses paid no attention and kept on walking.

As St. Peter finished giving President Bush the tour around heaven, they ran into Moses again, and St. Peter again tried to introduce President Bush to Moses, and Moses again ignored him.

Finally, St. Peter sought out Moses alone and said, "I don't understand. You're always so kind. Why did you ignore President Bush twice?"

Moses responded to St. Peter, "Look, the last time I talked to a bush, I ended up wandering in the desert for forty years!"

Laughter is one of life's greatest gifts to ourselves. Laughter is a mini-vacation. And if we would successfully cope with the stress and worry of life, then we all need vacations, we all need breaks, we all need some TLC, ASAP.

Alabama
"T.L.C. A.S.A.P."

PROBLEM THINKING

David Ball
"Thinkin' Problem"

Problem thinking is something we all struggle with. In David Ball's song, he couldn't stop thinking about his girl. In reality, obsessional thinking can be a problem for all of us. It does sometimes feel like our minds have a mind of their own, doesn't it? Instead of being our servants, our minds seem to be our master. We can't stop thinking about someone, or something, or some place.

When we face this kind of thinking we recognize that we are looking at the roots of addiction. We hear a lot about problem drinking, but in reality all drinking, and all addictive behavior, is first a matter of problem thinking.

The first thing we need to do is to step back from the problem and ask ourselves, "What am I getting out of thinking about this person?" In the case of the last song, the answer might be "I'm getting a lot of pain and misery out of thinking about this person." We then have to examine whether we think we're supposed to be miserable and suffering. In other words, any time we are hurting ourselves, there is some prior thought which justifies the hurt. For example, we may suffer from low self esteem, and think we deserve to hurt. We may think, unconsciously, that we really don't deserve to be happy. Maybe we feel guilty about a relationship and are trying to punish ourselves. There's one piece of wisdom that I have learned over the years in counseling, and that is that most of us grow up and duplicate our family of origin. In other words, if we grew up in misery, anxiety, depression, and so on, we will find a way to make ourselves miserable, anxious, and depressed, even when we have the freedom to make things better.

So, the first thought to making ourselves better, to stopping our problem thinking, is to examine what irrational assumptions and beliefs we carry in our heads. The beauty of life is this: if we have the power to hurt ourselves with our thoughts, we also have the power to make ourselves better and happier by changing our thoughts. As the great psychologist William James said, "The greatest discovery of this century is that by changing our thoughts we change our world." If we're unhappy with what we think, then we can think of someone else!

Patty Loveless
"I Try To Think About Elvis"

Changing our thinking is harder than we first imagined. We actually get addicted to painful thinking! In other words, when we have thought about something, hundreds or thousands of times, our brains begin to encode grooves, or paths, psychologists call them tapes, that play almost automatically. It's not easy to reprogram ourselves, but it is possible.

One step is to realize that we are not just putting words into our brains, but we are also making pictures. Patty Loveless tried to turn her thoughts to other things or other people in her song, but in her mind she was still making a big picture of this one man. If you are trying to let go of a person, or a hurtful memory, literally take a black and white photo of that person in your mind, and shrink it down to the size of a dot. You may have to do that dozens of times, but eventually your brain gets the message, that you are no longer making a big deal of this person. Then, after you have shrunk this other person down to a tiny dot in your mind's eye, begin to make a large, color picture of yourself being happy. Then each time you think of the hurtful person or event you want to let go of, take a black and white photo of that person or event in your mind, shrink it down to the size of a dot, and then replace it with a large, color, happy image of yourself. The message you send to your brain and to yourself is that you can be happy without this person or thing. People pay thousands of dollars to be trained in doing what I have just described. It works. We can reprogram our brains.

Another approach to problem thinking is to change our behavior. In other words, if we begin to look happy, to act happy, to exercise, we begin to feel better. Our feelings follow our behavior. Many depressed people have discovered that they cannot exercise vigorously and feel depressed at the same time. Another man changed his thinking by praying. As he put it: "I prayed for my boss Monday through Wednesday and everything went well. Thursday I didn't pray for him, and we got into a big fight at work." A wise person summed up changing our thinking by changing our behavior in this way: "Wear a smile on your face, a prayer on your lips, and hope in your heart. This food for the spirit helps you keep on climbing." However, it's always hard to go up, if our thoughts are always dragging us down.

Reba McEntire
"She Thinks His Name Was John"

Of course, we all have problems at times, and often we have problems with our thinking that conditions us for life. The important thing to remember is that we can change if we want to. The next thing is to realize that the change won't happen instantly. Some people can use the exercise I gave a few minutes ago, and change their thinking immediately. Others need years and years of private counseling. It doesn't matter. We can change and grow at our own pace and in our own way, but we can change. Usually, the only problem to being happier, healthier, more joyful in our lives is our own stubbornness. We sometimes cling to our hurtful memories and depressed feelings like a dog clinging to a bone. I saw a little saying recently that read: "God said He would work with stubborn people, but He didn't know there would be this many."

In Reba McEntire's song the girl who thought the boy's name was John is a sad example of someone who stubbornly defined her life by a loss. Near the end of the song, Reba sings that even her friends would say "what a pity, what a loss," even they got caught up in the drama. In reality, she may have been treated unfairly. She may have been hurt. But her life did not end. However, if she keeps dwelling on the negative, keeps thinking about the betrayal, keeps living in a state of feeling helpless and hopeless, then what she has done to herself is far worse than anything he may have done to her. All of us are victims of other people's hurts and cruelties. However, we don't have to stay victims. We can decide that we are going to treat ourselves well, even if someone else treated us poorly; we are going to make something good of our lives regardless of what someone else has said to us, done to us, or thinks about us; we can decide that God made us to enjoy and live life to the fullest, not stay stuck in sadness and self-defeating thinking and behavior. In all of my counseling with grieving people, I'm always aware of the principle that grief is a process and recovery is a decision. We need to take time to grieve, perhaps months or years, but we also must make a decision, at some time, to live again.

If we have lost a child, a parent, some relative or loved one, the way to honor their life is not to make ourselves miserable, but to honor their lives by living our lives to the fullest. If some tragedy has taken a loved one, like a drunken driver or a murderer, honor their loss by working to save the lives of others by joining Mothers Against Drunk Driving, or working to reform the legal system. Life boils down to this: "What we are against weakens us. What we are for strengthens us." If we spend our lives being against someone who has hurt us, then we doom ourselves to depression and anger. If we dedicate our lives to bringing as much joy and peace wherever we are, then we guarantee ourselves a life of joy and peace.

By a life of joy and peace, I do not mean a life of ease. I mean that despite the trials and tragedies of life, there is in us a quiet place where we feel joy and peace. We do have the power that those prisoners in a concentration camp had, who gave away their last piece of bread to another prisoner. We can, in any set of circumstances, choose our attitude and choose our behavior. We do not have to live like clowns who smile over sadness, and paint happy looks over sad lives.

Dwight Yoakum
"Pocket Of A Clown"

Life is not just what happens to us, but what we do with what happens to us. Life can be harsh and cruel, but we can choose to respond, not by becoming bitter and depressed, but by becoming better—more compassionate to the pain of others, more forgiving of the failings of ourselves and others, more determined to make life better for others.

I like to reflect on a little meditation called "Reforming Oneself," reprinted below:

It has been raining again. I have been indoors, meditating on the shortcomings of life. I wish there were more kindly persons in the world. Our competitive life develops selfishness and unkindness. I am determined to do something about it. I cannot hope to convert many persons. If I convert one person, I will have done well. I will begin with the person I know best-myself. Let me think. How shall I make myself kind, gentle, considerate? Wait a minute. I believe it has stopped raining. Now I can go out and do something. I won't bother to reform myself today. Perhaps tomorrow. That is, if it's raining, and I have to stay indoors and meditate on the shortcomings of life.

The moral is simple: we all wish others were better. We all delay making ourselves better. And yet, the truth is that if we change ourselves, we change our world!

There is a little beatitude that reads "Blessed are those who are FLEXIBLE for they shall not break." Like trees that bend in the storms but do not break, we need the wisdom to know that there is more to us, and to life, than we see. There is God with us, helping us to change the pictures in our mind's eye, helping us to change the thoughts in our brains.

If you have trouble letting go of the past, remember this little meditation:

Have courage for the great sorrows of life
And patience for the small ones;
And when you have laboriously
accomplished your daily task
Go to sleep in peace. God is awake.

We need to give the past to God with all its regrets, and live in the present. If you want new enthusiasm for the day, you might try this morning prayer:

Good Morning, God. You are ushering in another day, untouched and freshly new. So here I come to ask you God, if you'll renew me too. Forgive the many errors that I made yesterday. And let me try again, Dear God, to walk closer in your way. But Father, I am well aware I can't make it on my own. So take my hand and hold it tight for I can't walk alone.

The word "gospel" means good news. The good news is God's news, the news that God has come to save us. There are times when we feel helpless to change our thinking, or to change our lives. It's then we need to believe that we can do all things in Christ who saves us. We can choose to live in gratitude each day for what we have, not in regret for what we do not have. We can choose to be people who encourage others, not people who feel heavy for others to be around. We can choose these new attitudes because God is with us, helping us. With our lives, then, we can announce good news, and with our lives we can make good noise, the good noise angels once sang to announce the presence of God with us. "Glory to God in the highest, and peace to God's people on earth."

John Gorka
"Good Noise"

LAUGHTER

Often the
Best Medicine

TITLES OF OUR TIMES

As I begin my twenty-second year on the radio, I am still amazed at what God can do. While my show, "The Country Road," airs locally in Baltimore every Sunday morning and evening, it is carried across the country on about one-hundred stations, and broadcast around the world on Armed Forces Radio. (I never did receive my combat award, even though my voice was sent to the Persian Gulf!)

In case you've missed my show, allow me to name the kinds of songs you might also have missed. Titles of country songs tend to get right to the heart of the matter, which, as I already noted, usually has something to do with cheating, hurting, drinking, falling out of love, or falling in love. Rest assured, most of the following songs are *not* played on upstanding country-western radio stations.

♪ "Jesus Loved The Devil Out Of Me"

♪ "How Come Every Time I Itch I Wind Up Scratchin' You?"

♪ "Just Makin' Love Don't Make It Love"

♪ "We Used To Kiss On The Lips, But Now It's All Over"

♪ "I'm Gonna Drink Canada Dry"

♪ "I've Got You On My Conscience, But At Least You're Off My Back"

♪ "I Ain't Sharin' Sharon"

♪ "Get Your Biscuits In The Oven And Your Buns In The Bed"

♪ "I Don't Know Whether To Kill Myself Or Go Bowling"

♪ "You're The Reason Our Kids Are Ugly"

♪ "My Wife Ran Off With My Best Friend And I Miss Him"

♪ "If Fingerprints Showed Up On Skin, I Wonder Whose I'd Find On You"

♪ "You Can't Have Your Kate and Edith Too"

♪ "Let Me Love The Leavin' From Your Mind"

♪ "Don't Squeeze My Sharmon"

♪ "You're Out Doing What I'm Here Doing Without"

♪ "I've Been Roped And Throwed By Jesus In The Holy Ghost Corral"

♪ "Thanks To The Cathouse I'm In The Doghouse With You"

♪ "I Forgot To Remember To Forget You"

♪ "I May Be Used, But Baby I'm Not Used Up"

♪ "Too Much Of Not Enough Of You"

♪ "Now I Lay Me Down To Cheat"

♪ "We Just Live Here (We Don't Love Here Any More)"

♪ "Loving Here And Living There And Lying In Between"

♪ "Drop Kick Me Jesus Through The Goal Posts Of Life"

POSTMARKED "HEAVEN"

Teachers often send me notes and letters that their pupils write. The honesty and wit of children is quite sharp, and to envision their minds working out concepts of God is truly a joy. Children give some of the world's wisest philosophers and theologians a run for their money.

Here are snippets of letters from fourth and fifth graders at Bishop John Neumann School in Baltimore:

Dear God: How old are you? When did you stop making things?

Dear God: Why did you have to make us?

Dear God: Why did you invent my bratty sister?

Dear God: If you made the world, who made you?

Dear God: How is Roland doing up there? Can I come up?

Dear God: Why did you make rocks? All they do is sit still. They probably don't even sit.

Dear God: Why does my brother bug me so much?

Dear God: Why is the sun so bright because it hurts my

face?

Dear God: How come you made school? How come we could not play all day?

Dear God: Do you color birds with crayons or markers? And how come my mom talks on the phone for forty-five minutes?

Dear God: Why is the Red Sea called the Red Sea when it is blue?

Dear God: Is it true that when people die they come back to earth like in the movie "Ghost"?

Dear God: Is there a lot of people in heaven?

Dear God: Why can't people be friendly and not start wars all the time?

Dear God: How many years did your dad be a carpenter?

Dear God: Is there a reason you invented birds?

Dear God: Is there really a gate to heaven? Is Mary waiting at the back door? Is there a heaven?

BIG WONDERS, OR BIG DEALS?

Do you want something to help put your problems in perspective when you start yearning for "the good ol' days"? Let me offer a list of things we take for granted that the world did without for most of its existence.

In a book entitled *I'll Buy That* (and I *did* buy it!), *Consumer Reports* magazine detailed fifty small wonders and big deals that revolutionized the lives of consumers. We can debate whether the world is better for all these inventions, but there can be no debate that the world is forever different. You decide whether the world is better or worse in the wake of these wonders and big deals.

Air conditioners. Year-round climate control took the heat out of the change of seasons, fostering the development of the Sunbelt.

Air travel. In a little more than half a century, an eccentric transportation alternative for the hardy, privileged few became a fact of life for almost everybody. An old photo showed a co-pilot serving lunch!

Antibiotics. Before these microscopic warriors were discovered even the nicks and cuts of everyday living could be life threatening. The advent of World War II speeded penicillin to the marketplace.

1959 Austin Morris. British designers introduced a sideways engine and front-wheel drive.

Automatic transmissions. With one less pedal on the floor board, driving was suddenly a skill everyone could learn.

Black and white TV. Revolutionized entertainment, journalism, and advertising.

Color TV. Many believed no one would want it.

Credit cards. Francis McNamara in 1950 was embarrassed that he didn't have enough money to pay for dinner at a restaurant. He invented the Diner's Club card.

Detergents. Try getting clothes, dishes, and hair clean with plain soap.

Disposable diapers. If you don't remember what it was like to rinse, soak, wash, dry, and fold dozens of cloth diapers a week, ask your mother or grandmother.

Fluoridation. Tooth decay has been sharply reduced by fluoridating water supplies and toothpaste.

1965 Ford Mustang. The idea of the car as a personal toy came of age with this model—sports car styling and look of an affordable price.

Frozen foods. The ultimate convenience, if not the ultimate in nutrition.

Health insurance. Until Blue Shield, major medical problems often forced people to accept charity...or go bankrupt.

1942 Jeep. The wartime workhorse introduced us to four wheel drive.

Latex paint. Before this invention, you hired a painter. Now you do it yourself. Is this progress?

Magnetic tape. Brought tape recording into the home.

1949 Oldsmobile/Cadillac V-8. Big, powerful touring sedans ruled the roads for more than two decades.

Paperbacks. Made books available to everyone.

Pensions and social security. Provided, for the first time, minimum level of retirement security for working people.

Personal computers. What else can I say?

"The pill." I'm not going to say anything!

The polio vaccine. A dreaded crippler and killer of children was virtually eradicated, thanks to the discoveries of Drs. Salk and Sabin.

Power mowers. With them, we conquered the suburbs.

Running shoes. William Bowerman used his wife's waffle iron and some urethane to invent the Nike sole!

Fast food. Not ideal, but cheap, reliable, and predictable.

Suburbs. Where we moved to from the cities.

Supermarkets. Changed how we eat, shop, and cook.

Tampons. Originally denounced as a threat to morality.

Toyota Corolla. Started the Japanese invasion.

Transistors. Opened a new era of consumer electronics.

Transparent tape. Remember paste, glue, string, thumb tacks?

1951 Volkswagen Beetle. A real people's car.

Washers and dryers. Took the backbreaking work out of laundry. "Men know that the washboard, at best, is a killjoy, and at worst, a moving stairway to the grave," said Thomas Edison.

SAINTS AND SOAPS

By now, fellow pilgrim of the country road, you realize how important I think a good sense of humor and an ability to laugh are for one's physical and spiritual health. If that's the case, then there must be particular patron saints through whom we can petition a smile. Here are some such saints who come to mind.

For shoppers - St. Francis de Sales
For lawyers - Our Lady of Good Counsel
For firefighters - St. Blase
For fisherman - St. John Fisher or St. Polycarp
For chocolate milk drinkers - St. John Bosco
For bald people - St. Hedwig
For necklace wearers - St. Bede
For weight watchers - St. Josephat
For candy makers - Our Lady of Mt. Carmel
For bridge builders - St. Bridges
For campers - St. Coleman
For police - St. Procop
For travel agents - St. Martin of Tours
For knitters - St. Casimir
For winemakers - St. Anthony Claret
For gardeners - St. Theresa the Little Flower

And here is my often requested "Soap Opera Prayer," so

let us bow our heads and grab our remote controls.

O God, *As The World Turns*,
help us to remember that you have said:
"You are *All My Children*."
As your children, we ask you to be our *Guiding Light*,
whether we live in *Santa Barbara*,
or spend time in a *General Hospital*.
Since we have only *One Life to Live*,
may we realize that life does not belong
to the *Bold and the Beautiful*,
or *The Young and the Restless*,
but to those who are *Loving, All The Days of Our Lives*.
Bless us through all *Generations*,
and lead us to *Another World* with you.
Amen.

LANGUAGE

The Power of the
Spoken Word

CHOOSING WORDS WISELY

Hal Ketchum
"Every Little Word"

Life is literally what we make of it. We can choose to re-member the tender words of parents, spouses, and friends, or we can hang on to hurtful remarks, cutting comments, and put-downs. If you tend to hang on to injurious com-ments from other people, remember the good advice one woman offered: "What other people think of me is none of my business." What a freeing comment! She simply chose not to mind what others said. They were welcome to their opinions, but she was welcome not to listen to, or worry about, their opinions.

Think of the wasted hours remembering a hurtful com-ment. Think of the tears shed because of what someone said or did not say. Think of the hurt of remembering how we were misunderstood. In reality, other people's opinions of us are beyond our ability to control. Even Jesus could not control what others thought of him! However, he didn't hang around where he was not wanted. "Shake the dust off your feet," he said, "and go on to the next village." If we do not feel respected and appreciated where we are, it's okay to go where we are respected and appreciated.

Hal Ketchum's song "Every Little Word" reminds us how tender and caring words can bring joy. When I think of that song, I recall the last stanza of a poem:

> The three sweetest words: I love you?
> Wrong by heck.
> The three sweetest words are:
> Enclosed find check!

I'm joking, of course! Our life is made more beautiful, or more hurtful, by the words we speak, hear, and choose to remember. Words spoken in love, however, are our favorites.

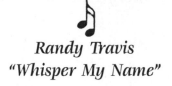

Randy Travis
"Whisper My Name"

The power of words can create beauty and peace and harmony. We cannot control what anyone else may say, but we can choose not to take to heart insults or hurtful criticism, and we can choose to say healing and helpful things to others. Some people are remembered just for smiling. I remember a parking lot attendant greeting everyone with a cheery "hello" and a smile as they left the lot. I recall a man in a wheel chair in front of a nursing home who would sit on the lawn, waving to the cars going to and from work. Someone else might have sat inside and felt they couldn't do anything. This man sat and waved, and surprisingly, a lot of cars honked and the passengers waved back. It's a rare person who does not appreciate a kind act or word.

In all my years as a priest, I've heard a lot of people say that they don't want any more pain, but I've never heard anyone complain about receiving too much love. Instead of undeserved criticism or nasty put-downs, try instead being a person who encourages, compliments, says helpful things. If we simply dedicated our lives to affirming other people, to encouraging other people, to seeing the best in others, we would all have a full-time job and a full-time joy.

When I think of the words we use, I think of the old story of the man who bought a horse. The previous owner said, "Now this is a very religious horse. He will break into a gallop if you say 'Thank God' and will only stop if you say 'Amen.'" So the new owner climbed aboard and said, "Thank God," and the horse broke into a gallop. As the horse raced toward the edge of a cliff, the rider kept shouting, "Whoa, whoa!" But the horse kept on galloping. Just before the horse and rider went over the cliff, the rider remembered the command and shouted, "Amen!" The horse immediately stopped just short of the cliff's edge. With sweat pouring off him, the rider looked down hundreds of feet below, mopped his brow, and said "Thank God."

Boy Howdy
"They Don't Make Them Like That Anymore"

People tend to create images and thoughts in each others minds. "They don't make them like that anymore" creates an image of a beautiful car or girl. We make important things big and bright and beautiful in our minds. Without realizing it, we are constantly creating pictures in our minds. If we are depressed or unhappy, the odds are good we are creating gloomy pictures, hurtful scenes, repeating negative thoughts in our own minds. How can we erase such images from our mental chalkboards?

One technique is to imagine a black and white picture in your mind of a hurtful scene, and shrink that picture down until it disappears. Then create a positive, happy, cheerful picture of yourself feeling good, or succeeding, and enlarge it. Keep this happy picture in front of your mind's eye. It's amazing how this simple technique works wonders in our moods.

A second thing is to watch our verbal diet. As a wise person said, "If we talked to others the way we talk to ourselves, we wouldn't have a friend in the world." We need to stop our self-criticism, our self-deprecating thoughts, and to think positive thoughts: "I am a good person. I feel good about myself. I can do all things through Christ who strengthens me." By feeding ourselves positive thoughts, perhaps thousands of times a day, we begin to change our inner reality. It is not reality itself that affects our mood, but how we perceive that reality.

Remember that story about the twin boys, one a pessimist, the other an optimist. One year the parents decided to see if they could alter their personalities, so for their birthday they gave the pessimist wonderful gifts and gave the optimist a box of horse manure. The little pessimist opened all his wonderful gifts and complained about what he didn't get, what was wrong, why he wasn't happy. Meanwhile, the little optimist opened his box of horse manure and started to smile, and said, "Where there's this much manure, there's got to be a pony somewhere."

Clint Black
"Half The Man"

Words help create our inner realities. "Life is not what happens to us, but how we react to what happens to us," a wise sage once said. In "Half The Man," Clint Black was able to appreciate the love given to him, and make something of himself. Another person may have received the same love, and failed to appreciate it. Jesus said that some people have eyes and do not see, and ears and do not hear. In marriage counseling, it is so important to help people see that they may not have failed to love, but their partner may not have been able to receive love or appreciate it. Again, the key in life is that we can only do and say what we can do or say. We can't control how someone else will perceive or respond to what we do or say.

When I think of making mistakes in judgment, I think of the farmer looking up at a man floating to the ground. The farmer exclaimed, "Say, you're a mighty brave guy to come down in a parachute in the middle of a hurricane." The stranger replied, "I didn't come down in a parachute. I went up in a tent!"

In life, we often see what we are conditioned to see. Someone who has been abused or abandoned or hurt early in life, is likely to be suspicious of others. These people often sabotage their own relationships because they cannot see real love because of their past conditioning. They need to get into therapy in order to become aware of this conditioning and begin to build new associations. They need to hear words of healing, words of insight, words to heal the inner child and the inner shame. In life it is not enough to cry. We need to get to the source of our hurt and begin to discover joy.

Rick Trevino
"She Can't Say I Didn't Cry"

We can use words to hurt ourselves and others, or words to begin to heal ourselves and others. The one fact remains true—we are usually our own worst enemies. In other words, someone else may have indeed hurt or injured us, but we can choose to seek counseling, can choose to think differently of ourselves, can learn to speak kindly to ourselves, and create bright, positive images of ourselves that literally change how we picture life. Reality is not just what happened to us. Reality is what we chose to do with what happened to us.

One of the most difficult pains to cure is the pain of regret. We often look back and remember what we did wrong or failed to do right, and spend the rest of our lives criticizing ourselves. We need to stop that. Some healing words I found that helped me are the words of a simple poem entitled "It Might Have Been Worse" by philosopher G.J. Russell:

Sometimes I pause and sadly think
  Of the things that might have been,
Of the golden chances I let slip by,
  And which never returned again.

Think of the joys that might have been mine;
  The prizes I almost won,
The goals I missed by a mere hair's breadth;
  And the things I might have done.

It fills me with gloom when I ponder thus,
  Till I look on the other side,
How I might have been completely engulfed
  By misfortune's surging tide.

The unknown dangers lurking about,
  Which I passed safely through
The evils and sorrows I've been spared

Pass plainly now in review.

So when I am downcast and feeling sad,
  I repeat over and over again,
Things are far from being as bad
  As they might easily have been.

Powerful thoughts! We need to forgive and be kind to ourselves in order to be forgiving and kind to others. We need to watch the diet of words we feed to others and to ourselves. If we are angry at ourselves because of investments we did not make that would have made money, we need to congratulate ourselves for being prudent and cautious with money. There's simply no proof that we would be happier with a billion dollars. If we said an unkind thing, now we have time to say kind things. If we did a hurtful thing, we have time to do healing things. We can't change the past, but we can choose to see the good we did in the past, instead of dwelling on the wrong, and we can choose to make something of our present and future.

Words have power. We speak of Jesus as the Word of God. If we let the Word of God into our hearts, if we sincerely live by loving God, and loving others the best we can, we can be sure of God's blessing. The worldly wisdom is "if at first you don't succeed, try, try again." There is wisdom to perseverance and will power. The Bible, in Psalm 95, however, suggests that "if today you hear His voice, harden not your hearts." Will power will not replace God power. Ultimately, it is not what we will, but what God wills, that matters. When we listen for God's voice, and then add our will to doing his will, we have an energy and a force that no one can stop.

As the great St. Augustine said, "Do what you can do, and pray for what you cannot yet do." If we learn to speak affirming and encouraging words to ourselves, we will discover that we more easily affirm and encourage others. St. Julie Billiart, the foundress of the Sisters of Notre Dame de Namur, wrote that "as the sunflower turns always to the sun, so should we turn always to God." When we turn to God, we find that we have a power to love a little stronger, a love that not only pleases others, but a love that pleases God.

♪

Diamond Rio
"Love A Little Stronger"

PROMISES, PROMISES

John Michael Montgomery
"I Swear"

"Promises, promises." So goes the cynical old saying, implying that what is said will be done has a poor chance of actually getting done. Vows are so easy to speak and so hard to live. In the moment of romance, we can't imagine living without this other person. In the moment of pain, we wonder how we can live with this other person! And that is the point of vows. Vows are a statement that we will be together because of our promises, our ideals, our values, and not our feelings. Feelings change. Promises do not.

In our society of disposable things, we too often have disposable relationships. We think that if the feelings are gone than love is gone. In reality, just the opposite is happening. Love begins when we love unconditionally, when we think of the other person, not just of ourselves. A wise counselor once commented that the marriage vows are really a promise to befriend each other for life. Friends may not always be hot lovers, but friendship endures long after feelings fade.

Couples that divorce often find that divorce doesn't work

either. Two people may no longer live together, but if there are children, their lives will be intertwined for as long as they live. They can still argue over custody, over money, over religious upbringing. Most divorces result in lower standards of living, less freedom, and all kinds of social complications. Couples who divorce still find themselves together at first communions and confirmations and bar mitzvahs and weddings. A paper may say they are divorced, but the children will keep them in contact. And the contacts are constant reminders of what might have been, constant sources of arguing, constant sources of social embarrassment. How important it is to discover that the journey of life is not about changing someone else, but about changing ourselves! A new boss, a new spouse, a new job will not magically make life better. What makes life better is a new me! Change may scare us, but love is worth taking the chance to do scary things.

Joe Diffie
"John Deere Green"

Sometimes it is easier to risk our lives spray painting our love high on a tower, than it is to risk our lives being faithful to the person we promised to love. Carving our initials in trees, painting our love messages on walls, getting tattoos, are often impetuous things. Yet, can't we decide each day to keep our love alive? Can't we look at each other and see the good instead of the disagreements? Can't we make an effort to remember what attracted us? Can't we list the things we like about our spouse, instead of dwelling on the negatives? Can't we make an effort to praise, to compliment, to show appreciation and respect to our partner on a daily basis?

A man who worked in a nursing home said that when he asked elderly people if they regretted anything, rarely did they express regret over something they had done. Most regret was expressed over things they had not done. Playing it safe may not always be the best way to live. Yet, according to one psychologist, we are conditioned to play it safe. "How many times do we say goodbye to our children with the words, 'Take some chances today!' Usually, we say something like 'Be careful' or 'Take it easy.' We create the idea that the world is fearful, rather than create the idea that life is an adventure well worth the risk."

When I think of love and risks today, I think of the story of the newly-married young professor who got a job at a local community college teaching a course in sex. He was a little embarrassed about telling his new wife that he was teaching a sex course, so he told her he was teaching a course in sailing. One night his wife showed up at the school to go out with her husband after the class. As she stood outside the classroom where her husband was teaching the class on sex that she thought was a class on sailing, a young woman came out. "Oh," the young woman said to the young wife. "Your husband is such a great teacher." His wife replied, "I'm really surprised. He doesn't know much about the subject. He only tried it twice. The first time he got sick and the second time he fell off."

Joe Diffie
"In My Own Backyard"

We often learn too late to appreciate what we had in our own backyard. The source of so much unhappiness is that we keep looking at someone else's yard, at someone else's spouse, at what someone else has or does. We often compare ourselves unfavorably with others. We often glamorize what others have. We may have chosen to be teachers or police officers and we compare our lifestyle to another couple who may have chosen to be doctors or lawyers. The key to keeping perspective in life is to keep our values.

Make a list some time today of the most important values in your life. What is most important to you: freedom, money, love, God, faithfulness, hard work, and on and on? Once you list your values, then make a list of what activities you have that will lead to fulfilling those values. If you list freedom as your first value, then marriage may not be for you. If you list fidelity as your first value, then commitments to God or community or a marriage partner may well be for you. Each of us has to list his or her own values. Each of us has to measure his or her own life by those values. Comparing ourselves to others is a study in futility because you may have chosen to live by other values. A monk and CEO, for example, will have very different values!

When I think of being faithful to values, I think of one of the most wrenching true stories I ever heard. A young woman, just out of nursing school, went to work in a poor inner city hospital because of her desire to serve the poor as Jesus did. One night, as she left the hospital after a sixteen-hour shift, she was attacked and brutally raped by five men. The woman and her family spent an entire year in psychotherapy, trying to heal from the trauma. It was not enough. The woman was so damaged by the experience that she hanged herself.

The father then did the hardest thing any man could do. He went to the prison and forgave the five men who had raped her. When others asked him how he could possibly do that, the man replied, "They could take my daughter, but I would not let them take my freedom. I would not let their behavior lower my values." He could have acted on his feelings of rage. He could have acted on his thoughts of revenge. Instead, he chose to act on his values, and his belief in God. Without faith in God, promises make no sense, in this life or the next life.

Merle Haggard *"In My Next Life"*

Fidelity to our farm, or fidelity to our spouse, may not have produced the results we wanted. The reason why Merle Haggard's song is so sad is because the man valued himself by the results rather than by his efforts. None of us can always control the results of our efforts. We can't control the rain, the snow, the heat, the attitudes of others, the results of our planting. Rather than bemoan what did not happen, he could have credited himself with not having given up. As a sagacious person once said, "The highest form of holiness is to never give up." He also had a right to feel good about his marriage. He had not made his wife rich financially, but he had made her rich in love. She stayed by his side at the hour of death. A lot of rich and powerful people have not had such a faithful spouse.

To be happy in life we have to redefine success, not by somebody else's standards of power or money or influence, but by our true standard—staying faithful to our values no matter what the cost. When Mother Teresa was asked about the thousands of people she helped, but also about the millions of people who died that she could not help, she replied, "We are not called to be successful. We are called to be faithful." Success is not numbers. Success is fidelity. A woman once saw a man throwing starfish from the shore back into the ocean to save their lives. She asked him what good it did, since so many hundreds of other fish were dying on the shore. The man replied, "It sure makes a difference to the starfish I saved!"

The key to happiness in life is to realize that each of us has been called to do something wonderful in life, to fulfill our mission in life, to leave the world a bit better. Yet, many of us are not sure what that destiny is. Joe Paterno, the long-time football coach at Penn State, once commented, "God gave each of us a destiny, and then he confused us with free will." I like that powerful little line. The best way to test if we are following God's call is to listen to the quiet voice of intuition, our conscience or higher self. I like to focus on the following poem, the writer's name escapes me, as a point of reflection:

Some strive for power but often in vain,
Some thirst for glory, so hard to attain.

Some crave possessions that wealth alone brings
But alas these are transitory things.

The wise are they who while on earth's sod
Seek first in their lives the kingdom of God.

Being faithful to our promises to ourselves is known as integrity. Being faithful to our promises to God is known as faith. Being faithful to our promises to others is known as commitment. We don't have to do anything that would violate our integrity, weaken our faith, or violate our commitments.

Tanya Tucker
"We Don't Have To Do This"

We don't have to break our promises. We don't have to follow the crowd, care what others think, or do what others do. God did not create us to be followers, but to be originals. When we are faithful to what is best in us, we are faithful to God.

When I think of being faithful, I recall a true story of a father and son who used to go away together once a year to a retreat center called St. Joseph's in the Hills, near Malvern, Pennsylvania. This was a special weekend that both men looked forward to in their adulthood. In the company of about three hundred other men, they would spend the weekend praying, listening to talks, going to the sacrament of reconciliation, and attending daily Mass. Eventually the son married. One day the father said something hurtful to the son's wife, and for five years neither the father or son spoke to each other. Both, however, continued to go on the same retreat, but one stayed in one end of the building and the other at the opposite end.

One day, the son went to see the retreat director, who was a priest, and told him about the hurt with his father. He asked the priest what he should do, and the priest replied, "I think you need to go to your dad and be reconciled to him. I know his room number. Here it is."

The next day, the priest saw the young man and asked him if he went to his father's room to talk. The young man said, "no." The priest replied, "I'm sorry to hear that. I think the Lord wanted you to reconcile." The young man replied, "You didn't let me finish, Father. You see, as I was walking across the campus to my father's room, I saw my father walking across the campus coming toward me. When he got to me he knelt down on his knees before me and asked for my forgiveness. I then knelt down before my dad and asked his forgiveness."

The following year, the priest saw the young man and

asked him how his father was. The young man replied, "Father, six weeks after my dad and I reconciled, he died of a heart attack. I can't thank you enough for helping me to listen to what the Lord wanted."

What a story! Maybe we have broken promises of trust with parents, friends, relatives, spouses, and on and on. Life is too short to hold grudges. Life is just long enough for love. If you have wronged someone, be big enough to apologize. If you have been wronged by someone, be big enough to forgive. Not to forgive someone who has hurt you is to go on hurting yourself. Victimized once, you make yourself a perpetual victim by holding on to the pain.

Our promises were made to be kept. Ask God to help you keep your promises. God can bring parents back to children, spouses back to each other, neighbors back to neighbors, friends back to friends. God's love amazes us. We amaze ourselves when we see the miracles of healing we can perform when we are willing to be forgiven, and are willing to forgive others. God kept his promise to stay with us, an amazing promise. Can we remake our amazing promises to stay faithful to each other?

John Berry
"Your Love Amazes Me"

SPEAKING AND LISTENING

Suzy Bogguss
"You Wouldn't Say That To A Stranger"

We seldom regret what we do not say. Too often, when we're angry, we try to hurt someone else, especially our spouse. One of the most important lessons we can learn in life is to fight fair. How do we do that? First, state what it is that upsets you—what incident, what words that bother you—and deal with that. Second, use the "I" word. "I feel hurt when you do this." "I feel angry when you say that." By beginning the sentence with "I", you are telling your spouse or friend your feelings. You are not blaming him or her. As insignificant as it sounds, saying "I feel angry when you do this" can be heard. Saying "You make me angry" will not be heard. Blaming turns another person off. Announcing your feelings helps the other person to hear. A third thing in fighting fair, in addition to sticking to the particular issue, and using the "I" word, is to not attempt to hurt your partner.

Too often, people confuse expressing anger with trying to hurt someone else, trying to punish someone. Hurting someone else just guarantees that the other person will get angrier, and be less likely to hear you. The reason we treat strangers so well is that we don't feel as comfortable taking out our frustrations on them, as we do on a spouse. It's sort of crazy, isn't it? The person we promise to love for life we use as an emotional punching bag, but we treat complete strangers with respect.

In addition to learning better forms of communication, we also need to learn self-control. We don't have to let what happens outside of us upset us! Imagine, for example, that while waiting at a traffic light, the car behind yours runs into your car. Your first reaction may be anger at the person in the car behind you. But as you get out of your car, you discover that the car at fault was pushed into yours by a car behind it—a chain reaction. Immediately, your anger at the person behind you ceases. We can learn to control ourselves, to think before we speak, to talk rather than get violent, to try to understand and help the situation, rather than react and try to hurt someone else.

Sometimes, then, we get into trouble for what we say. Other times we get into problems because of what we do not say.

Travis Tritt
"Foolish Pride"

When thinking about what we say and don't say, we realize we can get into trouble by refusing to apologize. Pride is a deadly sin because pride can separate us from each other, and can separate us from God. Saying "I'm sorry" is a sign of strength, not of weakness. If we have said or done something wrong, it takes courage and integrity to admit it. "I was wrong" may be one of life's shortest sentences, but it can save marriages and families.

I recall a true story of a man telling a priest how angry he had been at his father. The man had such a grudge against his father that he even refused to attend his father's funeral. "We hadn't spoken in twenty years," the man said. "I wasn't about to show up at his funeral!" "That was quite a grudge," the priest commented. "What were you so angry at each other for?" The man paused, and after an embarrassed silence, said, "I forget what it was." What a tragic story, but what a great parable of foolish pride. A family was torn apart permanently by some incident, an incident that was forgotten, but the grudge continued.

I'm not suggesting we stay within a relationship that is toxic, that is physically or emotionally or spiritually abusive. I'm not suggesting we play the role of the victim, blaming ourselves, forgiving someone who continues to hurt us, excusing away the perpetrator's behavior. However, once the hurt has ended, once the abuse has stopped, once we have protected ourselves against further abuse, then not forgiving the perpetrator simply hurts ourselves. "The thing wrong with an eye for an eye is that everyone ends up blind," Martin Luther King said so well.

When I think of things we don't say, I recall another true story of a boy who was asked in religion class, "Where do bad people go after death?" The answer the teacher was looking for was "hell." The boy remained frozen and speechless. After class, the teacher asked the little boy, "I know you knew the answer. Why didn't you say it?" The little boy replied, "My mommy told me not to say words like that."

There's wisdom in the boy's answer. When you are tempted to say something mean, ask yourself, "Would I say something mean to a child?" Only a disturbed person would say "yes." Yet, as adults, we treat each other brutally and cruelly, forgetting that every adult was once a child, that every adult carries a wounded child inside. Hurtful people

145

need to be resisted and stopped. No one needs more hurt in life. When we realize that what we do to the least person we do to God, it suddenly puts life into perspective. To say something hurtful, or not to say something helpful, is to steal dignity from someone else.

Bobbie Cryner
"You Could Steal Me"

Some things that sound seductive are really just stupid. "You could steal me," Bobbie Cryner sings. "You can commit the perfect crime." Yet, however seductive the woman in the song is, what she said is dishonest. Two wrongs don't make a right, most of us learned as children. In asking someone else to steal her, she was really refusing to take responsibility for her own life. Sadly, people will often use an unhappy relationship as an excuse to have an affair. This may lower the hostility level, since at least one person is having his or her needs met outside the marriage. However, it can be lethal for the marriage. It is far better to be honest, to work to improve a marriage, and not have an affair. It is far better to see a counselor for help, than to see a lover for lies. "To thine own self be true, or you cannot be true to anyone," Shakespeare said a long time ago. If counseling doesn't work, if your partner does not want to work on the relationship, then a divorce may be the only answer. At least, however, one relationship is ended before another is begun. The new relationship is at least based on honesty, and has some chance of success. Relationships that begin illicitly rarely succeed. He who cheats with you is likely to cheat on you.

On a lighter note, when I think of being honest in what

we say, I recall the story of Sister Susan who received ten dollars in the mail from her family. Not wanting to keep the money, the nun looked out the window, and spotted what looked like a homeless man on the street beneath her convent window. Quickly grabbing an envelope, she wrote "Don't Despair" on the outside, signed her name, put the ten dollars inside the envelope, and called to the man. He looked up, and she threw him the envelope. He picked it up, looked at it quizzically, and walked away. The next day, he returned to the convent with an envelope stuffed with money. "Here you go, Sister Susan," the man said. 'Don't Despair' won, and paid fifty to one."

Collin Raye
"Little Rock"

Eventually, the time does come to say something. In the last part of "Little Rock," Collin Raye sings: "I don't know why I kept it all inside. You must think I never tried." Sadly, when we hide our feelings, no one else can know what we feel. If we're sad and don't show it, someone may think we are cold and distant. "How can you be so indifferent at a time like this?" Often when someone is depressed or sad, we think that behaving cheerfully and trying to joke will help. It doesn't. It just further alienates us from the depressed person, who thinks we really don't know or care how they feel. We're better off just holding a depressed person's hand. Just being with him or her, simply listening.

But once Collin Raye began to be honest, to rebuild his life in Little Rock, then he was able to talk. Life is difficult, but not nearly as complicated as we sometimes make it. The four basic rules of communication are so simple. First, ask yourself "What am I feeling?" There are only a few basic feelings—sadness, joy, anger, depression, happy. Second, share your feelings: "I feel sad" or "I feel happy." Our partner is not a mind reader. We can't expect him or her to guess our feelings. Third, share your feelings without blaming. No one wants to be blamed, and almost no one hears or accepts blame. Blaming is a waste of time if I am trying to communicate with someone. Fourth, listen without judging. Nothing turns off honest communication quicker than someone making us feel wrong for our thoughts, especially by saying, "You shouldn't feel that way." That sentence turns off more communication than almost anything we can say. Instead, say something like "Oh, I'm sorry to hear you feel sad" or "Can I do anything?" or "Can you tell me more?" These remarks will let the person know you heard him or her, and encourage them to continue talking.

As with all communication, saying what we want does not guarantee that we will get it. Saying what we want simply means we respect ourselves more because we know we are worth asking for. Jesus told us that "your Father knows what you need before you ask," but he told us to ask anyway.

Tim McGraw
"Don't Take The Girl"

Sometimes, what we say to God—our prayers—often confuse us. I remember a businessman commenting that he tried prayer once, but it didn't work. What he was really saying is that he did not immediately get what he wanted. I believe, however, that every prayer is heard and answered. It may not be answered in the way we want it, or on the time schedule we set up, but it will be answered. And the answer we get will always be as good, or even better, than what we ask for. We may ask for continued earthly life; God may grant eternal life. We may ask for a healing for an injury or illness; God may grant the courage and strength to cope with the disability. We may ask to win the lottery; God may help us to be grateful for what we have. I'm reminded of the story of the man who prayed for wealth, success, and fame in his early years. As he grew older, he gave away all his possessions and went to live as a hermit. When he died, he asked God why he had not been granted wealth, success, and fame. God responded, "Well, you were a good man, prayed daily, kept all the commandments, and loved your neighbor as yourself. You certainly deserved all those things you asked for. But I loved you too much to give them to you."

Our world-view changes when we realize that God may love us too much to grant what we request, as opposed to thinking God does not hear or care when he does not answer prayers the way we want. A wise foreigner, commenting on the demanding way many Americans pray, once said, "In your country, it is considered a miracle when God does man's will. In my country, it is considered a miracle when man does God's will."

The real challenge in life is not what we say or don't say to God. The real challenge is listening to what God does or does not say to us. Listening to God's will for us is vastly more important than us imposing our will on God. Life is short. "Am I doing, or have I done, all that God has asked me to do?" is the proper question to ask. With sports, entertainment, work, and all the distractions of daily life, we protect ourselves from thinking about ultimate questions. One day, however, the biggest question will not be whether our team won, whether we saw the latest movie, or whether we got the job we wanted. Someday, "Have I done in life what God wanted me to do?" will be the biggest question. In order to help us keep perspective in life, remember these words by John McLellan in "The Crown and the Crocodile": "One day a group of people will go to a cemetery, hold a brief service, and return home. All except one; that one will be you."

♪

Confederate Railroad
"Daddy Never Was The Cadillac Kind"

A WAY WITH WORDS

Some people have a way with words. Have you ever been amused at announcements which didn't come out quite the way they were intended?

For example, a priest friend of mine remembers seeing in an obituary, "There will be a massive Christian burial..." No doubt the writer was instructed to print, "There will be a Mass of Christian burial...," but they heard it differently. I can only wonder what was going through the editor's mind: "Wow, those Christians are dying like crazy. There's a massive burial scheduled."

It reminds me of a time when I was visiting a hospital that listed Catholic patients by parish. One of the parishes was named, "St. Isaac Job." I can only imagine some secretary thinking, "Boy, these Catholics are strange. They either think Isaac had a last name or Job had a first name."

Another famous bulletin announcement concerned a church that announced on the following Sunday at 2 p.m. baptisms would be conducted in the front and the back of church. The announcement continued, "Babies will be baptized at both ends."

Another announcement around Easter time read something like, "The Ladies Auxiliary will be giving Easter eggs to all the children of our parish. At the offertory, Mrs. Jones will come forward and lay an egg on the altar."

Another intriguing announcement read, "Our parish is

interested in starting a 'Young Mothers' Club. Those wishing to become young mothers will please see Father Smith in his office."

An announcement frequently used in the Prayer of the Faithful also often comes out the wrong way. Instead of, "For the sick of our parish...," what comes out is, "For those who are sick of our parish, let us pray to the Lord."

One of my favorite mispronunciations in a scripture reading was the lector who read the passage about the suffering servant in Isaiah. The passage reads, "He did not turn his face from the buffets and the spittle." What came out, however, was "He did not turn hid face from the buf-fay." Now that's my kind of savior. Someone who likes to eat! Maybe if the pope had written an encyclical on "girth control" instead of "birth control" it would have been much more popular.

One of my favorite cookbooks was one containing Elvis Presley's most-loved recipes. It was entitled *Are You Hungry Tonight?*. Considering what happened to poor Elvis, I can't imagine why anyone would want to eat what he ate!

During typical Baltimore summertime heatwaves, people frequently ask, "Father Joe, can't you do something about the weather?" I always respond with my stock answer, "Sorry, I'm in sales, not management."

One summer I was privileged to conduct a weekend "camping" retreat at Blue Ridge Summit with some wonderful people from Our Lady of Hope parish. While I worked with the adults, a couple of wonderful youth ministers worked with the young people. One of their projects consisted of making crosses out of dough and painting them. At a touching moment in the liturgy, these crosses were given to each participant. Inspired by this scene, I managed to comment, "This is likely the only time in your life that you'll leave a church with more dough than when you entered."

WORDS THAT WOUND, WORDS THAT HEAL

Billy Ray Cyrus
"Words By Heart"

Words do hurt. We can know the words by heart, but that doesn't always take away the hurt. The old expression that "the pen is mightier than the sword" was simply a way of stating that words are mightier than the sword. Words have challenged people to revolution. Words have inspired courage. Words have resulted in terrible atrocities. The old expression that "sticks and stones can break my bones, but names can never hurt me" has not proven to be true either. We can remember cruel things said to us in childhood. Those words can still affect us in adulthood.

Words have power to hurt, and a wonderful power to heal. A wise person has said that "nothing improves hearing like a compliment." If you want to build up your children's self-esteem, let them overhear you praising them to someone else. A word of encouragement can help someone pass a test, win a game, change their lives. If we spent our time building people up instead of tearing them down, what a wonderful world it would be.

Each of us everyday can be an avenue of God's grace to other people. We have the power each day to let God speak through us, and we have the power to get in the way of God. Our choice in life is whether we will speak God's story or our story.

Collin Raye
"That's My Story"

What we say, obviously, says a lot about who we are. As Collin Raye sings, "That's my story, I'm sticking to it." Some people confuse stubbornness with strength. We are weak if we cannot tell the truth. In Raye's song, he revealed himself as a coward, hiding behind lies that fooled no one. Long ago a wise person said something to the effect that we always tell the truth, even when we try to lie. In other words, our words may say one thing, but our behavior, our body language, our eyes will say something else. A woman, for example, almost always knows at some level when a man has had an affair. "He always came home, kissed me, talked to me, and then took a shower," one woman related. "This one night he just came home and went right to the shower. I knew something was wrong." He had not said anything verbally, but he had said everything non-verbally.

The sad part about telling lies is that people won't believe us even when we tell the truth. At the end of the song, Raye said some other things that were probably true, but they were no more believable than the lies. It's so much easier to keep our integrity than it is to lose our integrity and try to regain it.

When I think of words and affairs, I think of the story of the man turning eighty, and his friends decided to play some tricks on him. So they sent a young woman to his apartment, and when he answered the door, she opened up her coat and revealed that she was wearing almost nothing underneath. "What are you here for?" asked the eighty-year-old man. "I'm here for super sex," the attractive woman replied. "Okay," said the old man. "I'll take the soup."

Martina McBride
"Life #9"

Martina McBride's song is a good response to Collin Raye's song "That's My Story." "Don't tell me no stories, I don't want no lies," Martina McBride sings. When we lose people's trust, we have lost what really matters. We can forgive a person's behavior easier than we can forgive a person's lies. After all, we all make mistakes, even big mistakes, but mistakes are forgivable. Lies, however, break trust, and so we're not sure we can ever really have faith in this person again. The line "If she would just admit she did this to me, then I could forgive her," means that it wasn't the offense, but her lying, that drove him crazy." The same is often true in cases of medical malpractice suits. The relationship the doctor has with the patient is more important than what the doctor may have done or not done. Patients can forgive a doctor who simply made an error in judgment. But covering up provokes enormous rage.

When I think of being honest, even about our failures, I recall the true story of the professor asking a student if he cheated by copying another student's test paper. Humbly, the student admitted he did cheat by copying from his friend's test. "It's a good thing you were honest," the professor said. "You see, you even copied his name!"

Words bind us together. Interestingly, the Bible refers to Jesus as the Word of God. Even God reveals himself through words. We reveal ourselves through words, as well. The Word of God reveals God as loving, forgiving, kind, compassionate, and constantly leading us to a better life. Can the same be said of us? A good piece of advice about words is "think before you speak." Is this really what I want to say? Is it unkind? How would I react if it were said to me? Perhaps that's another way of saying that we seldom regret what we do not say!

Evangeline
"Let's Go Spend Your Money Honey"

If you think about it, it becomes clear that our every action was first a word, first a thought in a person's mind. Spending money is first a decision before it is an action. Words have power.

That's why it's so important to pay attention to the silent words we say to ourselves; words that we often aren't conscious of saying. "Oh, I can't do that." "I never have any luck." "I'm not smart enough." Often we are saying these things to ourselves without even realizing it.

Check your own attitude first thing in the morning. Do you let the day control you, or do you set your own attitude toward the day? Do you live each day as an unrepeatable event, or do you just think of it as another day? Do you greet the day with a sense of excitement, a sense that it's good to be alive? Without realizing what words we are saying to ourselves, we may be talking ourselves out of enjoying the day. It's the power of words. Our words have the power to turn a garden into a cemetery or a cemetery into a garden.

I remember years ago, walking along on a beautiful day, when all of a sudden a negative thought went through my mind, and I was depressed. I realized then that if a thought has the power to do that, then a positive thought could reverse the process. It's so important to check on the mental diet we may be feeding ourselves, often without ever realizing we are "pigging out" on unhealthy thoughts.

Words have the power to hurt. They also have the power to work miracles of love.

Joe Diffie
"John Deere Green"

As we think about the power of words, we realize that words have the power to move hearts and to change lives. Whether it's three foot letters painted in John Deere Green, or letters from the Gospel of John, words have power. I'm reminded of the saying: "Prepare and prevent, rather than repair and repent."

Words have power for good. When I give workshops on building self-esteem in children, I suggest things like: give them four compliments a day; catch them doing something good, and praise them for it; correct them, but don't criticize them; and teach them to accept compliments. Then, I suggest that all the things we do to build our children's self-esteem can be done for each other. Suppose we gave our family and the people we work with four compliments a day. Think how much happier our surroundings would be. Wouldn't the workplace be a happier place if we corrected where needed but didn't criticize?

Words, however, only have power if we act on them. As a humorist once said, "When all is said and done, more is

said than done." Too often, that is true. However, we can resolve to give power to our words by finding God who gives
power to our lives. An insightful person once observed that
"some people carry their religion on their backs like a bur-
den. Others carry it in their hearts like a song."

Religion, properly understood, ought to lighten our
hearts. We have a God who didn't come to get us, but a God
who came to be on our side. We have a God who didn't come
to condemn us, but who came to forgive us. We have a God
who didn't come to find out what we were not, but one who
came to tell us all we could be. In short, we have a God who
came to be in relationship with us. When the Word became
flesh, love took on flesh. Every time we love, then our words
take on power, and our lives take on meaning. There's no
doubt about it.

Neal McCoy
"No Doubt About It"

LOVE

God's Grace
and Our Gift

THE MEANING OF LIFE

Joe Diffie
"Third Rock From The Sun"

For some people, life has little meaning. We're just the third rock from the sun, a place where things go wrong a lot, a place where life just sort of happened. And yet, someone else can look at earth and realize that our location in space is just perfect, just the right distance from the sun to sustain life. Any closer, the planet would be a humongous Weber grill. Any farther away, the planet would be a giant snowball. But, sort of like Baby Bear's porridge, the earth is just right. Coincidence, or divine positioning? Nowadays, even scientists are open to the reality of God. As one person said, "In the '60s and '70s, scientists would say 'I don't pray. I'm a scientist.' Today, scientists say 'I pray because I'm a scientist.'" In other words, the more we discover, the more mystery we reveal. The more we know we do not know, the more we realize that all the laws that sustain life could not just happen by chance.

As we surrender to mystery we realize that "seeing is believing" is being replaced by "believing is seeing." If we believe something, we can make it happen in our own lives, and if we believe something, we can believe in something as big and wonderful as God. In her book *Embraced by the Light*, Betty J. Eadie describes her near-death, out-of-body experience during which she met Jesus. She said to herself, as the Lord embraced her in eternity, "Is this Jesus, God, the being I feared all my life? He is nothing like what I had thought. He is filled with love."

If we make love and service the basis of our lives, then we discover that love is the meaning of life. If we make self-ishness the basis of life, then we ask "What's in it for me?"

John Berry
"What's In It For Me"

Selfishness keeps us from knowing the meaning of life. "What's in it for me?" is not a good question to base a marriage or a life on. Yes, we do have to protect ourselves from abusive people, and from people who will use us, we have to love ourselves in the sense of protecting our self worth. At the same time, real love asks "What can I do for you?" Love focuses on the needs of the partner, not just on our own selfish needs.

The inability to think of the needs of others has led to so many divorces. The statistics on divorce are not pretty. Single-parent families are six times as likely to be poor and two to three times more likely to have emotional and behavioral problems than children from intact homes. Children of divorce are more likely to drop out of high school, become pregnant as teenagers, have weak relationships with their fathers and mothers, abuse drugs, get in trouble with the law and ultimately get divorced themselves. Barbara Dafoe Whitehead noted that more than a third of those children surveyed-largely middle class kids-suffered from depression and under-achievement five years and longer after their parents divorced. Children whose divorced parents re-grouped into step-families did even worse, experiencing greater emotional insecurity, less involvement with their parents and a significantly higher probability of physical or sexual abuse than their peers from intact families, or even stable single-parent families.

The "what's in it for me" attitude has created untold pain and damage for others. The answer to the question of the meaning of life is more love, not more selfishness.

Doug Stone
"More Love"

True meaning, the true essence if life, is found in more love, not in more stuff. As Doug Stone sings, "She needed more love and time, and less of things money can buy." I saw a cartoon that showed a husband looking for something special for his wife. He looked at fur coats, and realized his wife didn't want to kill animals. He looked at jewelry, and realized she was not into that. He looked at perfumes, and realized he didn't know what to buy. The last caption in the cartoon series showed his wife kissing him as he gave her a check for her favorite charity. Sometimes we don't need more stuff to clutter our lives. We need to give more love so that others can have a chance to have lives.

Loving others does not mean not loving ourselves. Jesus told us to do both, to love our neighbor as ourselves. Again turning to Betty J. Eadie's book, she writes, "We can recharge our own spirits through serving others, having faith in God, and simply opening ourselves to positive energy through positive thoughts. We control it. The source of energy is God and is always there, but we must tune him in. We must accept the power of God if we want to enjoy the effects of it in our lives." To put what she says in another way, we love ourselves when we do good for others.

If loving ourselves, and loving and serving others, is part of the meaning of life, then surely we need a healthy image of who God is. I like how Betty J. Eadie describes how meeting the Lord changed her fear into love. She writes:

> I understood how others had been instrumental in distancing me from God, though I felt no bitterness or judgment toward them. I saw how men and women in authority over me had become prey to negative energy and had taught belief in God through fear. Their aims were positive, but their deeds were negative. Because of their own fears, they were using fear to control others. They intimidated those under them to believe in God, to 'fear God or go to hell.' This prevented me from really loving God. I understood again that fear is the opposite of love and is Satan's greatest tool. Since I feared God, I could not truly love him, and in not loving him, I couldn't love myself or others purely either.

When we learn the power of love, then we learn the power of making dreams come true.

Clay Walker
"Dreaming With My Eyes Open"

The meaning of life is to know, love, and serve God and

others in this life, and to be happy with God and others in the life to come. When we discover the power of love, then we discover the power of making dreams come true, not only our dreams of life, but making come true God's dreams of what he wants us to do. Without a sense of our personal power to love and to make things happen, we can do what Clay Walker sings about—spending our whole life just dreaming. But with the knowledge that we have God's power to love, then we can join with God in creating a world of justice, love and peace.

What do we need to make things happen in life? How do we fulfill God's plan for us, and make our lives true lives of love and service? "The ABC's of Achievement" is a good place to start to understand. Someone else made up this list, but I have changed some and added my own ideas.

A is for attitude. Our attitude must be positive. If we live with an attitude of gratitude for what we have, and an attitude of doing all we can each day to spread love and joy, our lives will be successful.

B is for belief. We need to believe in God's love for us, and in what God calls us to do. Believing is seeing.

C is for courage. We need to set goals, and have the courage to try. There is no such thing as failure. Failure is someone else's editorial comment on our efforts. If we have the courage to try, we are already successes.

D is for discipline. We need a sense of self control to make things happen. We need discipline to keep out of our lives whatever discourages or weakens us.

E is for enthusiasm. Enthusiasm comes from two Greek words meaning "in God." We need to be in God to make things happen.

F is for fun. We need to have fun, not just in our time off, but to make our work a challenge, something we enjoy doing.

G is for goals. We have to know where we want to go. A map only helps if we have a destination.

H is for hope. Hope is a magic ingredient that sparks us into positive action.

I is for initiative. We need to try something, even if it turns out not quite the way we planned. We learn from mistakes.

J is for just. We must be just and honorable in all our dealings.

K is for knowledge. Knowledge is power. We need to acquire knowledge and to use it. The more we know, the more like God we are.

L is for love. Love is what life is all about.

M is for motivation. We need to be motivated to believe that we make a difference. Our life is about doing God's work.

N is for negatives. We need to keep the negatives out of our lives. As Wayne Dyer stated, "What we are against, weakens us. What we are for, strengthens us."

O is for optimism. We can do what we think we can do.

P is for practice. We not only need to repeat actions to do well, but studies have shown that if we rehearse mentally, if we visualize ourselves doing well, we will do well.

Q is for quality and quantity. These are the twins of achievement-your calling cards as a person.

R is for responsibility. Responsibility means doing the right thing because it is the right thing.

S is for self-esteem. High self esteem is critical for achievement. We will do as well as we think we deserve to do.

T is for toughness. The mental toughness that does not yield to discouragement and put downs.

U is for understanding. We need to understand ourselves and others.

V is for virtue. Virtue comes from the Latin and means strength. We must have the strength to pursue the morally excellent.

W is for winning. Winning is the reward for hard work and positive attitude.

X is for "eXtra" mile. We have to be willing to do more, to go the extra mile.

Y is for you. You must believe in yourself, and in what God calls you to be.

Z is for zest. The power and gusto you put into being the best you can be for God and others.

Those "ABC's of Achievement" are easy to recite, but hard to live. To achieve in life, we need to love and believe in the God who loves and believes in us. In *Embraced by the Light*, Betty J. Eadie uses the following paragraph to close her chapter on meeting God during her near-death experience:

> Now I knew there actually was a God. No longer did I believe in just a Universal Power, but now I saw the Man behind the Power. I saw a loving Being who created the universe and placed all knowledge within it. I saw that he governs this knowledge and controls its power. I understood with pure knowledge that God wants us to become as he is, and that he has invested us with god-like qualities, such as the power of imagination and creation, free will, intelligence, and most of all, the power to love. I understood that he actually wants us to draw on the powers of heaven, and that by believing that we are capable of doing so, we can.

To close, in my own words, believing is seeing and to be known as someone who loves is to be known as someone who knows the meaning of his or her life.

♪

George Strait
"The Man In Love With You"

FUN-LOVIN'

Lorrie Morgan
"My Night To Howl"

Fun must be part of all of ᴏur lives if we are to be healthy and productive. As Doctor Haim Ginott writes, "Happiness is not a destination; it is a manner of traveling. Happiness is not an end in itself. It is a by-product of working, playing, loving and living." Did you notice that of the four things, loving and playing were just as important as working and living.

Ironically, we often associate fun with what we do when we're not married. When we speak of marriage, we use expressions like "settling down," "being tied down with the kids," "sow your wild oats before you marry." We make marriage sound like such a serious, somber experience that it's no wonder that people want to be single again.

While marriage does indeed involve hard work and commitment, marriage is also meant to be fun. One of the first things that one priest asks couples who come to him with marriage problems is "What are you doing for fun?" Too often in marriage, we forget to enjoy each other, to keep doing the things that made us fall in love, to keep our sense of humor and enjoyment of love and life. We may howl differently as married couples, but we can still howl.

Speaking of "howlin'" reminds me of the story of two Indians who were sending smoke signals to each other. Suddenly, in the distance, a huge, billowing mushroom cloud appeared—the result of a nuclear bomb test! As the Indians watched the huge, billowing cloud, one Indian turned to the other and commented, "I wish I had said that."

Tim McGraw
"Indian Outlaw"

Over the years, many kids have had fun playing cowboys and Indians. Yet, as we have learned in real life, the Indians were often the good guys. As is usually the case, history is written by the victors. Today, we know that fun is not real fun if it is at the expense of someone else.

How do we keep fun in our life? By making a decision to have fun! Sometimes couples will say that they can't afford to hire a baby-sitter in order to go out. A good response is that you can't afford not to hire a baby-sitter in order to go out. Whatever the cost of a baby-sitter, whatever the cost of an evening out, it's a lot cheaper than a divorce, a lot cheaper than poor health from not getting a break, a lot cheaper than living marriage as an endurance contest. If we forget how to have fun as a family or as a couple, then it becomes easy to forget why we are a family or a couple. When asked to come up with a list of qualities that go into making a happy family, experts came up with the following list: love, commitment, respect, support, forgiveness, communication, spirituality, time together, traditions, and a desire to enjoy life as a family, rather than as individuals who happen to live together. We have fun if we decide to have fun, even doing something like dancing.

Shenandoah
"If Bubba Can Dance (I Can Too)"

Everybody has fun dancing. By and large, women seem to enjoy dancing. By and large, men seem not to enjoy it quite as much. I'll never forget a wedding I presided over years ago. I overheard the best man, who happened to be the groom's older brother, giving him advice about the wedding reception. The best man said, "Look, at the reception, don't forget to go around to all the tables and visit with everyone, and thank them for coming." The groom replied, "If I thought I could get out of having to dance, I'd go talk to the people at the reception here, and then go to someone else's reception next door!"

Brides usually beam during the first dance. Grooms, with rare exceptions, usually look like they'd prefer to be in front of a firing squad.

Dancing can be fun. In the Bible there are many instances of people dancing to praise the Lord. Square dancing and line dancing, country favorites, allows everybody to join in the fun, with individuals not really needing to bring a partner to the hoedown.

Fun should always be laughing with someone else, not laughing at someone else. Respecting others is the secret to being respected ourselves. To respect others is to value their human dignity, their uniqueness. If family members and friends can see each other as created in God's holy image, then it is easier to be considerate. Cruel words, thoughtless acts, belittling others, making fun of another, judging others harshly, all shut down communication. Here are six suggestions for building good friendships and good relationships:

Accept others as individuals. Don't try to control them, to make them what you want them to be.

Respect your own feelings and other people's feelings. Treat others as you would want to be treated.

Listen. Really listen. A good listener, who listens with acceptance and understanding, will have more friends than the good talker.

Be honest with yourself and others. If you pretend to be what you are not, you will never be at peace with anyone.

Don't assume someone else can automatically recognize your needs. Ask for what you want or need. Don't expect others to be mind readers.

Express appreciation, rather that taking others for granted. Thank someone else for driving, for inviting you, for going with you. Appreciation goes a long way in building good relationships.

If we follow those six rules, then we will discover that finding love is not so much of a gamble after all.

Clint Black
"A Good Run Of Bad Luck"

Gambling can be fun for many. Unfortunately, few people win, and many people develop addictions to gambling. So while visiting a casino in another state can be a fun trip, don't bank on winning to be your fun. If you take time to notice, you will see more people smiling as they go into a casino, than you find smiling on the way out of a casino.

Clint Black's song about gambling reminds me of a story about a man who taught his dog to play poker. As the dog sat at the table playing, one of the man's friends said, "That's a pretty smart dog you have there." The owner replied, "Oh, he's not so smart. Every time he gets a good hand, he wags his tail."

Another story that comes to mind is one about a priest visiting a prison one day, and a young inmate stopped the priest and asked if he would pray with him. The priest agreed, and the young man explained, "I'm not a Catholic, but I grew up right across the street from a Catholic church. Every Wednesday evening, I could hear the Catholics praying in the school hall. Can I say one of those Catholic prayers with you?" The priest said certainly, and the man bowed his head and began to pray: "B1...I16...N32."

Everybody, including Catholics, need to be able to laugh at themselves, and we're all familiar with the Catholic love for bingo. Bingo is one form of gambling that many do seem to enjoy. "If gambling was so bad," someone once said, "why did the apostles cast lots to pick the successor to Judas?" In life, we need to have fun, and to take it easy sometimes.

Travis Tritt
"Take It Easy"

Having fun does not mean using or abusing other people. The man in the last song had four women who wanted to own him and two who wanted to stone him. In reality, none of us were made to be treated casually. Casual sex produces casualties, not fun.

One of the really interesting lines in Travis Tritt's song

"Take It Easy" is "I got to know if your sweet love is going to save me." Ultimately, no human love is going to save us. We were saved once and forever by a divine love. As the Gospel of John (3:16) says so well: "God so loved the world that he gave his only Son, that whoever believes in him may not die but may have eternal life." God did not send the Son into the world to condemn the world, but that the world might be saved through him. Having fun ultimately depends on having a relationship with God.

Having fun entails enjoying life as it is, despite its heartaches and disappointments. As psychologist David Myers, author of *Pursuit of Happiness*, writes: "Happiness isn't found in a vague, distant future. It's in this morning's phone conversation with someone seeking advice, in this noon's meal with a friend, in this evening's bedtime story with a child."

For those seeking joy, happiness, and fun—in and with their families—I like to share this blessing, written by Dolores Curran:

> Bless our home and make it fit for you, O God.
> Send your Holy Spirit into each nook and cranny.
> Let the walls resound with love and laughter.
> Let your birds sing on your trees outside and your lilies flourish in the garden.
> Bless our kitchen and fill it with the warmth of shared bread.
> Bless our family room and fill it with loving communication.
> Bless our bedrooms and fill them with restful slumber.
> Bless each room and each of us, dear Lord, and make yourself at home with us.

Trust in God. Care for each other. Give life your best.

And your home and heart will know happiness. Put simply, if we do our best to make our relationships and our families fun, then we may never have to take them apart.

Tanya Tucker
"We Don't Have To Do This"

WHEN LIFE'S PHASES FAZE LOVE

Tim McGraw
"Down On The Farm"

One important phase of life is the adolescent time of just having fun. So often in our society today, there is so much pressure on teens to have a "steady"—to be dating one particular person—that we forget how to just enjoy the group. Down on the farm, young people were able to laugh and joke, enjoy the cars and trucks, and just enjoy each other.

One woman I know described her fondest memory of adolescence: "My favorite time in life was when I was dating a boy who just liked me, who didn't try to come on to me sexually, who thought I was smart and told me so. He was my best friend." Because of our society's obsession with sex, we too often forget how to be friends because we think we are supposed to always be lovers. In the safety of the group, boys and girls, young men and young women, can learn to enjoy each other as people, not as objects to be lusted after. The country can teach some wisdom to the city.

I recall, when visiting the Holy Land, that our guide pointed out the Bedouin tribesmen who stayed in the desert, raising sheep and goats. The guide explained that the

Bedouins were not poor, they could live in the city, but they believed that cities were bad because they were built by men, but the land and sky and sun and rain were from God. So they stayed in the desert to be close to God.

When I think of the wisdom of simple folk, I recall the farmer asking his son to go outside to see if it was raining. The son replied, "Why don't you just call the dog in and see if he's wet?" Well, there comes a phase in life when we do a lot of calling.

Garth Brooks
"Callin' Baton Rouge"

There is the phase when we break away from the group and fall in love with one special person. Nothing in life is as good as the time of falling in love. Both people feel excited, idealize each other, and think this person is the answer to his or her dreams. And each does a lot of calling. Men, who can hardly utter a word once they are married, hang on the phone for hours when they are dating. For men, the conquest—getting the girl, getting married—is important. Once they get married, men too often take the spouse for granted and focus on work or something else, whatever the next challenge or conquest is. The quickest way to fall out of love is to stop doing the things that made you fall in love!

When I think of falling in love, and talking for hours, I'm reminded of the story of the man of few words, who dated a young lady for years. Finally, one evening he asked, "Will you marry me?" The woman replied, "Yes." Then the young man just sat there blankly. Finally, the young woman asked, "Aren't you going to say something?" The quiet, shy man replied, "I think I've said too much already."

Two things can never be taken back—an arrow that has been shot and word that has been spoken. That's a wise old saying that reminds me of a story about the old Baltimore Colts football player Art Donovan. Once Artie threw a bucket of water at a player coming around the corner, only to realize it was the coach. Artie said, "I was chasing after the water, trying to get it back in the bucket." It's fun to party and play jokes, but we can wind up in a heap of trouble.

James House
"A Real Good Way To Wind Up Lonesome"

There's a time for partying as a group, then a time for falling in love with one special person. Finally, there's a time for settling down with that one special person. Unfortunately, some people have a hard time settling down. They want to continue to live life after marriage the way they did before marriage. They want to keep bar hopping, hanging out, acting single. While it is okay for a couple to have separate nights out, it's disastrous if one of the parties feels like the spouse finds others more attractive.

It's hard settling down. In fact, the phrase "settling down" sounds ominous, almost deadly. In reality, getting married doesn't mean life ends. It just means that life changes. We no longer live just for ourselves, but we consider our partner's wants and needs and feelings. That isn't always easy. It's easier to make our partner wrong, instead of taking the time to understand our partner's needs and wants.

Which reminds me of the story about the woman asking the judge for a divorce. "Do you have any grounds?" the judge asked. "Yes, your honor," the woman replied. "We have three quarters of an acre." "No," said the judge, "I mean, do you have a grudge?" "No," the woman replied, "but we do have a lovely carport." Frustrated, the judge demanded, "No, not that. Does he beat you up or anything?" The lady replied, "No, your honor, I'm the first one up every morning." Totally exasperated, the judge asked, "Why do you want a divorce?" The woman replied: "Your honor, that man simply can't hold an intelligent conversation!"

♪

Alabama
"We Can't Love Like This Any More"

There always comes some period of disillusionment. St. Ignatius, the great saint and spiritual director, referred to these times as desolation and consolation. We have to realize that both periods are a part of life. Life will not stay fascinating. Another person will not stay fascinating.

In Alabama's song, however, one of the lines spoken by the male character is "So where we go from here is in your hands." That's not a fair statement. A relationship is not the job of one person. It is the job of both people. A more honest statement would have been "What can we do to make life better? Is there anything I can do to help you feel better?" Relationships don't get better by withdrawing into ourselves and feeling sorry for ourselves. Relationships mature when partners talk about their feelings and work to do things differently. As the old saying goes, "If you keep doing what you've always done, you'll keep getting what you've always got."

Apart from what we can do to help our partner, we also need to realize that we must be personally happy in order for our relationships to be happy. Our partner is not responsible for our happiness. As Lillian Eichler Watson writes:

Real happiness is not dependent on external things. The pond is fed from within. The kind of happiness that stays with you is the happiness that springs from inward thoughts and emotions. You must cultivate your mind if you wish to achieve enduring happiness. You must furnish your mind with interesting thoughts and ideas. For an empty mind seeks pleasure as a substitute for happiness.

It can be a phase of wisdom in life when we realize that we are responsible for our own happiness, and we cannot make someone else happy. And it can be humbling to realize that what our partner does for happiness may not include us!

Tracy Lawrence
"I See It Now"

Going on with our lives after the loss of a love is one of the toughest phases. It's hard watching someone else get involved with another partner, or get remarried. It's especially tough if there are children involved. That's why again and again I beg married couples with children to do all they can to avoid divorce. Divorce does not simply mean that the parents no longer live together. It also means that, with both parties living separately, each will struggle financially. The children will have divided loyalties, the hurt and frustration will continue.

After a loss, we need to take time to heal ourselves. A

comforting little reflection about rebuilding our own happiness offers this prescription:

> Look upon what gives you joy. Speak to those who warm your heart. Listen to that which lifts your spirit. Do what makes you happiest. Surround yourself with sights and sounds and people who give you pleasure.

I like that little reflection because it helps us to come to grips with the fact that we have power over our lives, we have power to make ourselves happy by choosing our thoughts, being with people who are good to us, deciding to feel peaceful despite the things around us we cannot control.

Through all the phases of life and love, whether we work on our first relationship, or are rebuilding after various relationships, one critical reality is to believe that love is real, and commitments can be permanent. Not everyone will be unfaithful. Not everyone will hurt you. Not everyone will break your heart. There are no perfect people in this world, but there are good and decent and lovable people who do their best. So if you decide to marry, choose wisely, be adaptable and flexible in living, practice forgiveness, keep a sense of humor, and be determined to stay together and work out problems. Keep God at the center of your life and of your relationship. Do all this and your love can last a lifetime.

Alan Jackson
"Livin' On Love"

DECEPTIONS AND DELIGHTS OF LOVE

Travis Tritt
"Take It Easy"

When we deceive, we find little delight. The man in Travis Tritt's song apparently was good at deceiving women, but, in the end, paid for his deceit when four wanted to own him and two wanted to stone him. Only one was a friend. When we start deceiving, then we can't tell someone who loves us from someone who wants to use us. All the women that he had in that song reminded me of what someone said about the wise King Solomon, with his hundreds of wives. They said, "It's not hard to figure out why Solomon was so wise. It was because all those wives were giving him advice!"

When I think of deceptions in love, I think of the little poem that reads as follows:

> He met her in the meadow
> As the sun was sinking low.
>
> They strolled along together
> In the twilight afterglow.

Patiently she waited
As he lowered away the bars

Her soft eyes beamed upon him
As radiant as the stars.

She neither smiled nor thanked him
Because she knew not how.

For he was a farmer's boy
And she was a Jersey cow!

Well, as we think of love's deceptions, we realize that not only can we deceive others, but we can deceive ourselves. There are those who look for love and find pain instead, but they allow someone else to continually break a piece of their heart.

Faith Hill
"Piece Of My Heart"

Deceptions are worse when we deceive ourselves. Why do people stay in painful relationships? Usually, because they don't think they deserve better! Their lack of self-esteem often keeps them trapped. They often don't have the self-confidence to believe that they could make it on their own, nor do they have the self-worth to believe that someone else would want them. One of the terrible prices we pay for someone who keeps treating us poorly is that we keep thinking poorly of ourselves.

How do we get unhooked from our self-defeating pat-

terns? First, we must make a decision that we deserve better treatment, and that we are worth something. Then we
try counseling, read books, talk to friends, and hang around
with people who love and care about us. That last point is
critical. We can be counseled, learn new ideas, and get support from friends, but if we keep hanging around people
who devalue us, we will stay with low self-esteem. Keeping
our self-worth is a daily battle. We're worth the battle, but it
is still a battle. Advice does not always help. As a humorist
once said, "It is better to give than to receive advice." Never
take advice from anyone who has less to lose than you do.
It's easy for someone else to tell you to leave a relationship
or to quit a job, but you have to believe in yourself and in
your own worth. When you're going through dark nights of
the soul, their advice seems far away.

Life is tough. When we're going through deceptions in
love, we wonder, not only about someone else deceiving us,
but we sometimes wonder where we were.

Ricky Van Shelton
"Where Was I?"

There is little delight in being deceived. He wants to
know where he was when she decided she didn't love him.
Of course, the other side of the coin may be that she was
telling him, but he did not want to hear it. Denial can fool
us. Denial simply means refusing to see what I don't want
to see.

How do we stop deceiving ourselves? First, by listening
to what those who love us say. As someone once said about
drinking, "If others think you have a problem, you have a
problem." This doesn't mean we are always wrong and oth-

ers are right, it just means that, if we have built up a pattern of deception over the years, we will be the last to see our deception. The second thing to do to stop deceiving ourselves is to listen to those who don't like us! Ironically, those who point out our faults may well be pointing to areas of life in which we need to grow.

How do we become less deceptive with ourselves within ourselves? By finding basic, moral principles and measuring our lives against them. The ten commandments might be the best place to start. If we're breaking any of the commandments and pretending it's okay, we're deceiving ourselves. As we rebuild our lives, we need to rebuild the principles on which we base our lives. Here are four guidelines that one person suggested for better living: (1) Do every job as if you were the boss; (2) Treat everybody else as if he or she was you; (3) Drive as if all other vehicles were police cars; (4) Live every day as if it were your last. Think how much quality there would be in our work, how much better we would treat each other, how many fewer people would die in accidents, and how much better we would be, if we followed just those simple suggestions. One principle remains eternally true, and that is, until we know ourselves, we're not likely to know what's going on in anyone else.

Mark Chesnutt
"I Just Wanted You To Know"

When we miss opportunities to nurture love, the delights of love quickly pass. Regret is a terrible pain to live with. As a keen-witted person once noted, four things do not return: the spoken word, the sped arrow, time past, and the neglected opportunity. Sometimes we regret the chances we took. Most often we regret the chances we did not take!

Why do so many marriages and relationships fail? They fail because of stubbornness, our refusal to talk, and our unwillingness to change our behavior. Read and meditate on these few lines of poetry:

> Too much of wasted happiness,
> Too much of broken bliss,
> When friends will not be friends again
> And lovers cease to kiss.
> When moonlight calls to romance
> And romance will not hear;
> Too much wasted happiness,
> From stubbornness, my dear.

In life, our worst enemy is usually ourselves. We cannot control anyone else. We can only make ourselves the best people we can be. The best of us get fooled and manipulated in life, and all of us get fooled and manipulated in love. Many men can identify with the following verses:

> She took my hand in sheltered nooks,
> She took my candy and my books.
> She took that lustrous wrap of fur.
> She took those gloves I bought for her.
> She took my words of love and care.
> She took my flowers rich and rare.
> She took my time for quite a while.
> She took my kisses, maid so shy.
> She took I must confess my eye.
> She took whatever I could buy.
> And then she took another guy!

Deception is a part of life and love, but we can all recover. We can learn and become wiser. For one person who will take all our money from the bank, there will be another whose love is better than money in the bank.

John Anderson
"Money In The Bank"

Love's delights grow greater if we have survived past deceptions. It's so easy to get fooled in love, to marry a person who looks good but who is not good, to confuse lust with love, to project onto others what we want to see, rather than what is really there. But if we don't get discouraged by past hurts, we will find love that makes all the hurt worthwhile. We can wall ourselves off from human relations to avoid hurt, but that way we also avoid love. As a wise man commented: "Remember this, each man alone has the power to build his throne; and this fact is also true. He can build his prison too." Walls that we put up to protect us can also imprison us.

Love is worth the struggle, because only love has lasting worth. Money and power and fame never deliver what they promise. Remember this little poem the next time you're tempted to envy the millionaires:

> If I had a million dollars
> A good man said one day,
> My wish would be just to scatter
> Good cheer along the way.
> If I had a million dollars,
> I would say good-bye to care,
> And every night some glad one
> Would name me in his prayer.

One day by stroke of fortune,
The dream he dreamed came true.
They brought him a million dollars
From an uncle he never knew.
What of the noble impulse
The good man had before
He wore himself out in trying
To make a million more.

In the psalms there's a verse that reads: "The worthless are prized highly be the sons of men." We chase illusions in life. We deceive ourselves. But love is a delight when we meet the special person. Love is measured, however, not by what we find but by what we give. We need to be honest with ourselves and with others, and make promises that last for life. Society measures us by what we wear. But love is measured by the promises we swear.

John Michael Montgomery
"I Swear"

FALLING OUT OF LOVE (Part I)

Blackhawk
"I Sure Can Smell The Rain"

What makes a woman fall out of love? Falling out of love is not a sudden thing. We don't fall in love overnight. We don't fall out of love overnight. The man in the last song sensed something was wrong. That's the time to do something. Ask your wife: "Is something wrong? Can I do anything to make you feel better? Would you want to go to talk to a priest or minister or rabbi or counselor?"

The truth is that if you suspect something is wrong, then something probably is. Trust your intuition in matters of the heart. Women often get into trouble by not asking for what they want, by not saying what bothers them, by not being clear about what would make them happier. What too often happens in relationships is that both people avoid dealing with a problem when it is still manageable. By hoping that "something will happen," they almost guarantee that something will happen—the relationship will get worse!

When there is a problem, silence is never golden. Nothing makes a woman feel as unloved as being ignored. While men thrive on appreciation, women love respect. A woman needs to be talked to, to be listened to, to be praised and complimented. Taking a woman for granted causes her to cease to feel special.

Very often this is tough for men to comprehend. We get a lot of satisfaction from what we do, what we accomplish. The man in the last song possibly felt good that he was providing financially for his wife and family. Yet, income is not enough. I recall an old clergyman once saying that marriages would last if couples were "incompatible"—if he earned the income and she was "patable." In reality, that's not true.

An image I often use with men in seminars is that giving a woman a beautiful home gets one point. Bringing home a rose in a bud vase also gets one point! For most men that's mind-boggling. Men think that bigger is better. "I gave her a beautiful house, but she's never satisfied." The issue is not that she may not appreciate the house. The issue is that she still needs frequent small reminders that she is special. It's not a real romantic imagery, but sometimes it's helpful to remember that we don't fill the car with gas once a year! We fill it as often as necessary. The same is true with relationships.

Part of the frustration is that often the very things that make a woman feel good, are not all that important to men. We men often thrive on time alone, being in our cave, whether that's the cellar or den or garage, or whatever. While we like to be appreciated for what we do, we often forget that a woman will feel better if we just listen to her, spend time with her, let her know that we understand. A woman needs to feel respected, understood, and cared about. If she does not, then likely she will get angry!

Brooks & Dunn
"She's Not The Cheatin' Kind"

Falling out of love is a process. If a woman feels disrespected, uncared for, not understood or listened to, then she will be angry. Unfortunately, going out to have an affair because a husband had an affair, the theme of the last song, doesn't solve anything. That's known as acting out, rather than talking out.

We need to talk our hurts and feelings out, to let our partner know what upsets us, and what pleases us. We can't fix what we can't talk about. And women can help men by letting them know that they are part of the solution, not just part of the problem. If a man just hears blame, just hears put-downs, if he feels unappreciated for his efforts, then he will simply shut down. That's why most affairs have little to do with sex and everything to do with anger. No better way to hurt a partner than by cheating on them. Unfortunately, we also hurt ourselves and hurt our own sense of self worth. Affairs always increase the hurt and solve none of the problems. However, in our desperation, in our loneliness, in our hunger for affection, sometimes we mistake being desired for being loved.

Mary Chapin Carpenter
"Shut Up And Kiss Me"

The process of falling out of love for women is really a series of things: not feeling respected or understood; not feeling cared about or listened to; not being made to feel special and wanted. Very simply, the things men do to make a woman fall in love—take them out; compliment them; tell them how attractive they are; bring small gifts; spend time with them-we need to do to stay in love.

More deeply, though, beyond romance, we need to learn

to be friends again. None of us can always feel sexy or sensuous; none of us can always feel attentive and understanding. However, we can learn to be friends. C. Raymond Beran wrote a little reflection that describes friendship:

> What is a friend? I will tell you. It is a person with whom you dare to be yourself. Your soul can be naked with him. He seems to ask of you to put on nothing, only to be what you are. He does not want you to be better or worse. When you are with him, you feel as a prisoner feels who has been declared innocent. You do not have to be on your guard. You can say what you think, so long as it is genuinely you. He understands those contradictions in your nature that lead others to misjudge you. With him, you breathe freely. You can avow little vanities and envies and hates and vicious sparks, your meanness and absurdities and, in opening them up to him, they are lost, dissolved on the white ocean of his loyalty. He understands. You do not have to be careful. You can abuse him, neglect him, tolerate him. Best of all, you can keep still with him. It makes no matter. He likes you. He is like fire that purges to the bone. He understands. He understands. You can weep with him, sin with him, laugh with him, pray with him. Through it all-and underneath-he sees, knows and loves you. A friend? What is a friend? Just one, I repeat, with whom you dare to be yourself.

Divorces increase because men and women realize, often too late, that they need less sex and sensuality, and need more love and friendship. The old saying is true: We fall in love for many reasons, but we fall out of love for only one reason. We're not friends any more. The number of divorces today may not mean that marriages are any less happy. Today, however, women have more control over their fertility and their finances and consequently, no longer feel the need to stay in unhappy relationships. Power always brings options.

Most marriages, however, do work. The statistics that half of all marriages fail are simply misleading. Among Catholics, the divorce rate is about twenty-five percent—indicative of a church that encourages couples to consider all aspects of marriage before the "big day"; a church that offers marriage preparation; and a church that supports marriages through encounter movements and counseling. All of this indicates that if we work on marriages together we can make a difference.

Love ultimately is a decision. While no one should have to put up with abuse, we do need to believe in repentance, in changing, in being different. Consequently, any marriage that works will have to accept each other's shortcomings, forgive each other's sins, and appreciate each other's limitations.

One attractive, young woman said to me once, "I'm happily married, but I'm still waiting for the man of my dreams." She recognized that, while she would never divorce her husband, she did appreciate that he was no fantasy. And that was a sign of maturity on her part. Every girl deep down may yearn for Prince Charming, or some handsome person to carry her off on a white horse. Instead, every girl gets another human being. But, in accepting each other as we are, instead of making each other wrong for what we are not, we have the basis of lasting love.

Collin Raye
"Man Of My Word"

LOOKING BACK, TAKING STOCK

John & Audrey Wiggins
"Has Anybody Seen Amy"

The Wiggins' song reminds me of words written by a Scottish poet, who penned "My heart is a lonely hunter that hunts on a lonely hill." As we look back in life and in love we realize that what the Wiggins sing in "Has Anybody seen Amy" is true: "You can always go home, but you can never go back."

It's lonely going back because what we go back for is always gone. He was looking for Amy on one level, but what he was really looking for was his lost youth. As he watched the other teenagers, he realized that they listened to music with a similar beat, but the heart was missing. His heart and his love.

Leon Trotsky once wrote that "old age is the most unexpected of all the things that happen to a man." Aging is an interesting process. We realize that things don't stay the same because we don't stay the same. When I drive past places I used to play baseball, I wonder how we could have played a game on such a small field. I remember wanting to get a hit more than anything in the world, but to the cars going by it meant nothing at all. Age helps us understand that what we once thought was all so important is really mostly in our own minds. Someone once defined sports as "organized irrelevance." In other words, every sport has rules and regulations, and we cheer or yell, and yet ultimately, it doesn't really matter. The world is not really changed by any game. Aging helps us realize that things only have the importance we give them.

A woman who survived a near fatal accident never again got upset. When her adolescent children would be having all kinds of crises, she would just listen calmly. When friends asked how their mom could stay so cool, her teenage children would reply: "Mom sees the big picture." A near death experience puts life in perspective. Wisdom helps us to look back at what is and what is not really important. As the great English writer Somerset Maugham wrote, "The great tragedy of life is not that men perish, but that they cease to love."

Reba McEntire
"She Thinks His Name Was John"

Looking back can teach us to learn from our mistakes, or it can keep us in depression, paralyzed by our mistakes. The looking back that reminds us only of the hurt, that keeps us stuck in the past, that reinforces our identity as a victim, only further hurts us. Injured once, we injure ourselves again and again by looking back and remembering. We do need to take time to mourn, to heal, to help the inner child who got hurt. But we also need to move on if we're not going to destroy ourselves.

"Most people are not against you," someone wisely concluded. "They are for themselves." That thought, and Reba McEntire's tune "She Thinks His Name Was John," remind me of what Helen Rowland once wrote, that "nothing annoys a man as to hear a woman promising to love him forever, when he merely wanted her to love him for a few weeks." In other words, the "John" in Reba's song may just have wanted casual sex. The female character thought John loved her. That's why there really is no such thing as casual sex. If sex is not part of a commitment of care, it becomes hurtful. Instead of sex being put in the service of life or love, it simply reinforces another person's already poor self-image. Sex that is a part of love leads to joy. Sex without love leads either to shame or addiction or both.

When I think of how we search for that special other, I recall a pastor, as part of a fund-raising technique, promising to dedicate a hymn at the service to anyone who gave ten dollars. Immediately a young woman went to the altar, handed the pastor ten dollars, turned to the congregation, and pointed to a handsome young man and said, "I'll take that 'him.'"

Toby Keith
"Who's That Man"

Life can be painful. Women are not the only ones who get hurt in love. Men can also be treated unfairly and unjustly. As we look back, we realize we will make ourselves sick if we keep looking back. Like the man in the last song, we may need to look at what was once our home, feel our sadness and anger, and then drive on. The harder we resist tears the longer our sadness will hang on. The more we nourish our anger, the likelier we will do something we will regret. We may need to yell our anger out, cry it out, or talk it out, rather than act it out.

Once we have acknowledged our feelings, however, we have to let go. A big part of letting go is forgiveness. Many people misunderstand forgiveness. They say things like "You mean I have to let him or her get away with this?" So in their effort to do or say the hurtful thing, the revengeful thing, in hanging on to the hurtful experience, they punish themselves, trying to punish a former partner. Forgiveness is all about self-love. Do I love myself enough to set myself free from this experience? Forgiveness is the key to action and freedom. Once we forgive, we are no longer holding onto the pain. And once we are free of pain, we are free to do something for ourselves. Whatever we think about, whatever we focus on, will expand and grow. If I keep thinking about the hurtful experience, I will stay trapped. Hurt will flourish. If I forgive, I am free to live for now. My thoughts are free to build a new life, to think of new things. We can never go on to something better until we let go of something worse.

Alabama
"We Can't Love Like This Anymore"

There comes a time when repeating the past becomes intolerable. We can't love like this any more, because this just isn't love.

So often the root of staying stuck in the past is that we don't have self-confidence. I think most fear boils down to two basic beliefs. We either think *we* don't have what it takes—that we're not competent enough, not good enough, not able to make it on our own—or we think *God* doesn't have what it takes—that God won't be there to help, won't catch me if I stumble, won't pick me up if I fall. Believing in God begins with the simple statement: "Lord help me to believe." Then we follow up the prayer by going to a church or synagogue or other place of worship. By reading the Bible, reading other inspiring books, getting involved in a Bible study. To really believe, we need to belong to a community of belief.

To believe in ourselves, we need to believe we are made in God's image and likeness, and hence, we have all we need to make it in life. We need to say things to ourselves such as "Through God, I have all the power I need to solve my problems"; "I am talented and capable"; "I am creative and intelligent"; "I am a beautiful and competent person"; "I can turn problems into opportunities"; "I am a positive person filled with energy"; "I am forgiven!" This little set of affirmations may be a list you want to repeat to yourself a dozen times in the morning and hundreds of times throughout the day. We need to reprogram ourselves to look at our strength and goodness, rather than stay stuck looking at the past. Looking back and remembering our pains and putdowns can turn us into lifetime victims. Believing in God and in ourselves can turn us into victors! Life can be a tangled mess at times. We need to take some time to untangle our minds.

Clint Black
"Untanglin' My Mind"

There also comes a time to untangle or lives. Maybe a love relationship didn't work. It doesn't mean we are bad people. It just means we may have made a bad choice. We can improve ourselves, improve our decisions, get to know ourselves better, and make better choices in the future. We can change and be different if we believe we are worth being better to.

Here's a concise little formula for improving ourselves. As I said earlier, we get what we think about. Give yourself life-enhancing thoughts and pictures. Let go of the "if onlys" and "what ifs" of life. We only beat ourselves up with regret. Forgive people who hurt you, not only because God told us to do it, but because forgiveness sets you free to live in the present, not in the past. Remember these two sentences: "There is nothing to fear. There is always hope." Even if tragedy happens, God will be with us. Even if we die, God will raise us up. Try to live as Jesus suggested when he pointed to the lilies of the field. They don't worry or fret but God clothes them with beauty. We don't have to be running after clothes and stuff that the world runs after. Let God be in you, and be at peace with life.

When you are feeling low, instead of comparing yourself to people you believe are more successful, look at all the people who have less. Most of the people in the world would give anything just to live in the U.S. To improve your life, then, think of your successes, dream wonderful dreams, make plans that excite you, and expect your plans to come true.

We don't want to go back into the past if it just imprisons us with guilt, worry or self doubt. But, if we have discovered love, if we have learned to love God, love ourselves, and love and respect others, then we can heal the past by going back, and celebrating the love that makes our present and future beautiful.

Garth Brooks
"Callin' Baton Rouge"

FALLING OUT OF LOVE (Part II)

Brooks & Dunn
"That Ain't No Way To Go"

We previously examined some of the stages of falling out of love—anger, depression, denial, bargaining, and, finally, acceptance. "That Ain't No Way To Go" is about anger and denial. There is no easy way to break up with someone. One or both of the parties is bound to be angry. Talking it out is preferable to walking on out, but in the case of abusive people, in the case of people who refuse to hear, in the case of violent reaction, the other party may have to protect himself or herself. Ideally, we should try talking before separating, try counseling before divorcing, try praying together to become better at staying together.

Brooks & Dunn's song also highlights denial, with lyrics like "you left with no warning" and "can't believe my eyes." In reality, the woman in the song probably displayed many signs of unhappiness. However, no one is a mind-reader. It is important, especially for a woman, to ask for what she wants and say plainly what would make her happy. He may have been in denial. She may have been into her own anger—withdrawing in a hostile silence and planning on leaving. Sadly, some people would rather be right than happy. They would rather be right, convinced that a person is no good, than to try to improve things, to do things to make things better, to talk to the spouse rather than about the spouse.

On a lighter note, when I think about denial and anger, I recall the story of the little girl being put to bed for the night. A few minutes later she called, "Daddy, will you bring me a glass of water?" Her father replied, "No. Go to sleep." A few minutes later the little girl called again, "Daddy, would you bring me a glass of water?" Her father replied again, "No. Go to sleep." A third time the girl called out, "Daddy, would you please bring me a glass of water?" The father responded, "Go to sleep or I'll come up there and spank you." There was a short silence, and then the little girl replied, "Daddy, when you come upstairs to spank me, would you please bring me a glass of water?"

Tanya Tucker
"Hangin' In"

The stages of falling out of love are painful times. Tanya Tucker sings about her depression—"running out of reasons to be strong"—and she sings about denial—"hangin on 'til you're with me again." One antidote for general depression (not clinical depression that might require therapy and medication) is to simply make the decision to be happy again. Yes, we do have to take time to talk, to cry, to mourn, and so on. I often quote the saying that "grief is a process; recovery is a decision." Some behavioral analysts have discovered certain practical things to conquer the blues. For example, visualizing ourselves being happy, helps us to actually feel happy. Also, they have discovered that if you smile, you will feel better. Also, if you exercise, or just walk briskly, your mood will improve.

It takes work to get yourself mired in depression. We have to work at staying stooped over, at keeping our eyes downcast, at thinking only negative thoughts. But if we stand up straight, smile, look and walk with confidence, think good thoughts about ourselves, then our mood will lighten.

We are not victims of someone else's behavior. We may indeed miss someone else, but we don't have to punish ourselves by constantly thinking about the loss, or depressing ourselves by our bodily expressions or behavior. Diane Swanbrow, in an issue of *Psychology Today*, wrote that "new research reveals a surprising truth: the tendency to feel unhappy may lurk in your genes, but happiness is something you can create for yourself...The capacity for joy is a talent you develop largely for yourself."

Remember the old saying that God made you, and God doesn't make junk. If someone else has hurt us, there is all the more reason to be kind to ourselves. Because someone has rejected us, we don't have to reject ourselves. We don't have to blame ourselves for a failed relationship. True, we may have made mistakes, but it's better to learn from mistakes than just to brood over them. We did the best we could at the time, hopefully. And, despite our best efforts to save a relationship, it's probably true that love was gone before the person was gone.

♪

Carlene Carter
"Something Already Gone"

During the stages of falling out of love, there are different times to feel different ways. There is a time to be sad. There is a time to remember all the wonderful things that were—the good times, the falling in love times—and to let ourselves mourn. There is no time limit on grief. We grieve at our own pace. We mourn not only the loss of a person, but the loss of dreams, of hopes, of plans for a better life. I think of the story of the father asking his son which dog he wanted, and the little boy pointed to a puppy wagging his tail and said, "I want the dog with the happy ending." All of us want happy endings, but everything doesn't always end happily.

Joan Savio, writing in "Christopher Newsnotes," spoke of her sadness and her coping with sadness this way:

> When my husband died a few years ago, I felt like I wanted to die too. We were so close, so in love. How could I go on without him? I talked it over with God and told Him how I felt as I cried many tears. But God let me know that He wanted me to live because my work on earth was not yet finished. He reminded me that as much as I loved Donald, my life was separate from his. God was right, because although I still love and miss my husband, my best friend, I'm no longer unhappy because I'm busy reaching out, trying to do God's will for me. In the process of healing and growing, I have become a joyful and fulfilled person. Instead of giving up, I gave in, and became the person God wanted me to be. I'm sure God is pleased because others will now see His light shining in me and through me.

The stages of falling out of love are tough. One minute we are through with a person; the next moment we want to go back to that person.

Blackhawk
"Every Once In A While"

Making a decision to go or to stay is difficult. The important thing is to keep as many options open as possible. Some couples discover, for example, that separating for a time makes it possible for them to stay together. Each person may know the pain of the relationship, but neither may know the pain of loneliness. As one man replied, when he was told how lucky he was to be single and free, "I'm free all right. Free to go home alone. Free to cook just for myself. Free to come and go as I want because no one else cares!" He unmasked the fantasy of single life. There are those who like being single, and may want to spend their lives that way. There are others who want to be married. Love has a way of dividing sorrow and multiplying joy. A bad relationship may seem like hell, but a good relationship may be as close as we get to heaven in this life.

Sometimes, however, we have to admit that a relationship just won't work. At that point we need to make the best of a separation. If there are children, every effort should be made to avoid a divorce. Children seem to do better in households with two people, even two people who are not ecstatically happy all the time. If there are no children, or if the relationship is abusive, then separation may be the answer. Even Jesus said that there was a time to shake the dust off our feet and go on to the next village.

When I think of endings, I recall the story of the couple who was inspired by the "eeny, meeny, miney, moe" method of making a choice. So they named their first three children Eeny, Meeny, and Miney. When they were asked why they didn't name their fourth child Moe, they responded, "We didn't want any 'moe!'" Another bad pun, but in the stages of falling out of love, there comes a time when we don't want the relationship any more, when we don't stay awake worrying any more, when we no longer cry any more. That's how it feels to have fallen out of love.

John & Audrey Wiggins
"Falling Out Of Love"

The final stage of falling out of love is acceptance. There comes a time when our feelings have been spent, and we are ready to move on. Sometimes we wonder why it took us so long. As the Wiggins sing, "I look back and laugh at the fool I've been." We don't have to do that to ourselves. As a sign on the wall of an alcohol rehab center reads: "No one comes here too soon or too late." Whatever time it takes to get to a point of resolution is the right time.

Now is the time to get on with our life. Yes, we may think of the other person again. We may still have moments of anger and sadness. But coming to terms with loss means we learn to respect ourselves, to believe that we are worth living for, to know that if someone else left us we do not have to leave ourselves. Life is worth living, even if we live by ourselves. When we discover that life is worth living, it is only natural to want to share life with someone else.

Using a metaphor based on rules of grammar, William de Witt Hyde constructed the following reflection on life:

Live in the active voice, rather than the passive. Think more about what you make happen than what is happening to you. Live in the indicative mood, rather than in the subjunctive. Be concerned with things as they are, rather than as they might be. Live in the present tense, facing the duty at hand without regret for the past or worry over the future. Live in the singular number, caring more for the approval of your own conscience than for the applause of the crowd.

When we decide to live life, we then decide to make a difference in life. If one person did not love us, there are thousands of others who need love. We can do something with our life to help kids, to work with hurting adults, to assist the elderly. One of life's greatest cures for blue feelings is to do something for someone else. We may indeed experience pain in the future, but it won't be the pain of living in the past.

Steve Wariner
"It Won't Be Over You"

CHRISTMAS IS THE SEASON OF LOVE

Alabama
"Santa Claus (I Still Believe In You)"

The time before Christmas can be the best time of the year. Anticipation is often greater than the reality. At Christmas, we believe again. We believe in love again, in giving again, in seeing love in others again, in celebrating the best in us, and not dwelling on the worst in us.

A wise person said that there are three stages for believing in Santa Claus: believing in Santa; not believing in Santa; and becoming Santa. Christmas brings us back to our beliefs.

The key to living well during the hectic days before Christmas is to not let time rule us. We can get so caught up in the wrapping, cooking, shopping, decorating, and all the planning that we forget the meaning of Christmas, which is to celebrate the arrival of God as one of us. And this feast does not exclude anyone. Centuries of unhappy history has often divided religions. But Jesus came as Messiah for Jew and Gentile, not to divide the two. Jesus came "not to condemn the world, but to save it" so sincere people of all faiths who put their faith in God, follow their consciences, and love their neighbors are included in salvation history. At Christmas we celebrate the God who loves all in order to teach us to love all. A God who could bridge the gap between God and humanity can certainly help us bridge our human differences.

On a lighter note, Christmas is not just about bridging the differences years of prejudice have built, but about getting and giving gifts. Here's an old poem, by Arthur Guiterman, about gifts that has some wise and humorous advice:

> When Bill gives me a book I know,
>   It's just the book he wanted, so
> When I give him a ping-pong set,
>   He's sure its what I hoped to get.
> Then after Christmas we arrange
>   A little Christmas gift exchange;
> I give the book back to him, and he
>   Gives the ping-pong set to me.
> So each gives twice—and that is pleasant—
>   To get the truly wanted present.

A wise insight into Christmas giving, but to exchange Christmas gifts, we have to be home for Christmas.

Forester Sisters
"I'll Be Home For Christmas"

As we think about getting ready for Christmas, we realize we all want to be home for Christmas. For many, spending Christmas at home is usually a wish come true; for many others, it is often a wish unfulfilled. However, if we are able to love, then we can send love across the miles.

At Christmas time, we are more aware than ever of those who won't be home, those who have gone before us in death. I'll never forget a true story of a man who left Germany early in the 1900s, at age thirteen, to find work in South America, and later in the United States. He never saw his mother again because of the two world wars. One night, years later, he had a dream wherein his mother appeared to him. Years later, after World War II, he found out that it was exactly the night that his mother had died in Germany. I think even those who have died come home for Christmas, if only in our dreams. When I visited Bethlehem in the Holy Land, I felt closest to my own deceased mother. For her, heaven would be to dwell forever near the scene of Christ's birth. It would be fitting that she who exemplified the spirit of Christmas, the spirit of giving, should have heaven in an eternal Christmas scene.

People take holiday fun pretty seriously. At holiday time, we need to take our grief seriously, too. We may need to take time to cry, to be silent, to pray to and for those who have gone before us. Our hope indeed is that they are home for Christmas. We also need to work through our depression by caring for those who have less—the homeless, the families in shelters, the single parents who cannot afford an expensive Christmas. Giving to our families and loved ones is wonderful, but realizing that everyone is part of our family is even better. "Each one, reach one" is a wonderful expression. Suppose each one of us just reached out to help one person outside of our families? What a healing force Christmas would be to people around the world.

Christmas, then, evokes different feelings and emotions. While some of us dream of going home, others are pleading for others to come home for Christmas.

Ricky Van Shelton
"Please Come Home For Christmas"

Christmas touches our greatest joys and our greatest vulnerabilities. This can be a time of seasonal depression for those who dwell on their losses. This can be a time of seasonal hope for those who dwell on the deeper meaning of Christmas. If you anticipate that this will be a difficult Christmas because of a separation by death or divorce, then plan to celebrate Christmas differently. For years on Christmas eve I was part of an ecumenical group that celebrated a Christmas eve service just for the single, the divorced, the widowed, and the separated. Often even going to church is painful for those whose families are separated. This way we created a family of families. You might want to consider doing something like that in your community in the years ahead.

In addition to worshipping differently, don't be afraid to celebrate differently. If you think you might be alone for Christmas day, don't be afraid to ask a friend if you can drop by for Christmas. Don't be afraid or ashamed to ask for what you need. If you have an intact family, don't be afraid to look around for a single or separated person who might be alone for the holidays, and invite them to join your family. Hurting people are not just the homeless on the streets. Hurting people might be a newly divorced or widowed person down the street.

Again, while we try to focus on what we give for Christmas, many, especially the young, focus on what they might get. Every kid has dreams of what he or she wants. Every kid lives in fear of getting clothes, or some other "boring" gift. Let me share an old poem, which probably dates back to the '40s or '50s, entitled "Presents":

> I wanted a rifle for Christmas
>   I wanted a bat and a ball.
> I wanted some skates and a bicycle,
>   But I didn't want mittens at all.
>
> I wanted a whistle,
>   And I wanted a kite,
> I wanted a pocketknife
>   That shut up tight.
>
> I wanted some books
>   And I wanted a kit,
> But I didn't want mittens one little bit.
>
> I told them I didn't like mittens,
>   I told them as plain as plain.
> I told them I didn't want mittens
>   And they've given me mittens again.

Well, Christmas is a time of great expectations and small disappointments, and a time for past Christmas memories.

Alabama
"Christmas Memories"

Some Christmas memories, however, can make us cry. We think of good times with people no longer with us. We think of times of disappointment. The real spirit of Christmas is a spirit of hope, not pain. One little boy put it all in perspective when he was asked, "Did you get everything you wanted for Christmas?" The boy responded, "No, but then again, it wasn't *my* birthday."

One of my favorite Christmas stories is about a poor family living back in the 1950s. The parents were separated, the father had abandoned the family, the mother was alone raising four small children. The mother bravely tried to wrap up small gifts of socks or gloves to give the children something to open on Christmas day. But this year they were so poor they could not afford to even own a tree. About nine o'clock on Christmas eve, someone knocked on the door. A man was going house to house selling Christmas trees.

"I'm sorry," said the mother. "I don't have any money."

"What can you afford?" asked the man.

"I can't afford anything," she replied. "I only have a quarter."

"That'll be enough" the man said. And he gave her the nicest tree he had. For years that Christmas tree lived in the family's memory as the nicest tree they ever had.

Christmas is not about greed or getting all we can. Christmas is about generosity. It's about *giving* all we can. And while we cannot be equal in the amount we give, we can all be equal in our desire to give. The widow's mite was equal to the large donations of the rich. That was the message of Joseph and Mary's boy.

Alabama
"Joseph And Mary's Boy"

We need to remember what Christmas is all about—God coming into the world to set us free from prejudice and sin, to set us free from selfishness and domination, to set us free from just living for ourselves in order to be free to care about each other. The message of Christmas is that we are all brothers and sisters, all sons and daughters of the same father, all people bonded by a common creator, and all destined to build a common kingdom—a kingdom of justice, and light, and truth.

Christmas is not about God coming for just one group. Christmas is God coming as one of us to break down barriers that separate groups, so that we can be reminded that God is like all of us. So, one of the most important things we can do, especially during the bustle of the pre-Christmas season, is to wait for this love to enter our world, and then for that love to penetrate our hearts. Marchette Chute, in a little verse entitled "The Day Before Christmas," said it best:

> We have been helping with the cake,
>   And licking out the pan.
> And wrapping up our packages,
>   As neatly as we can.
> And we have hung our stockings up
>   Beside the open grate.
> And now there's nothing more to do
>   Except to wait.

In the days before Christmas, let us wait and let us realize that those who wait for the Lord are never disappointed. The loving God of all years will make this a loving time of year.

Travis Tritt
"Loving Time Of The Year"

THE POWER OF LOVE

Vince Gill
"When Love Finds You"

Love does many things. It can move mountains and make hearts beat faster. Love appeals to our ideals, and it helps us see what's ideal in other people.

One of the challenges of love is that sometimes we set up impossible expectations for love, which reminds me of the story of a minister who ran into a woman whose wedding he officiated. The minister asked, "Well, has your husband been faithful to all the things he said before you got married?" The woman replied, "He sure has. Before we married, he said that he wasn't good enough for me, and he's been proving it ever since!"

One person, as wonderful as he or she may be, cannot be everything to us. We need a life apart from our spouse as well as with our spouse. In other words, we need to balance our personal needs with our relationship needs. Each person needs to feel that he or she is the most important person in the world to the spouse, but that doesn't mean that both will not need other friends, other activities, other things to do and to learn. Sometimes in our efforts to control another person, we simply drive them farther away from us. Each person needs to say and do things that reassure the partner that he or she is still number one, but each person also needs to grow personally, to keep learning, to keep being interested in life.

Love is wonderful. Like an earthquake, it's the big one — it really shakes things up!

George Strait
"The Big One"

Love does have the power of an earthquake. Love helps to focus our energies, to motivate us, to give us meaning and purpose in life. Love helps us to move beyond ourselves and to see the needs of someone else. The truth of life is that love is so much more than romance, and so much more than sex. Don't get me wrong—romance is wonderful and sex can be great. As a couple I knew years ago said, "If God created anything better than sex, he kept it for himself."

And yet, God did create something better than sex. He called it love, and God did not keep it for himself. It was love that motivated God to create us, to stay in touch with us, to enter human history and die for us. Love is so powerful that the Creator fell in love with the creatures. We can understand something of God's love when we see the passion of lovers, and the commitment of parents to their children. Love is about giving, forgiving, caring and sharing. According to the words of St. Paul, "You are God's chosen race, he loves you, he has given himself wholly for you. You should be clothed in sincere compassion, in kindness and humility, gentleness and patience."

St. Francis of Assisi, who himself turned from romantic

love to love of God, wrote, "You have been called to heal wounds, to unite what has fallen apart. No one should be roused to anger or insult on your account, rather all should be moved to peace, goodwill, and mercy because of your gentleness." In other words, the great saints remind us that love doesn't just have the power to change us. Love has the power to change our world.

On a lighter note, I recall the millionaire groom promising a pastor that the size of his fee would be in direct proportion to the duration of the wedding service...the shorter the better! So as the couple stood before the minister, he looked at the bride and asked, "Take him?" He looked at the groom and asked, "Take her?" Then he looked at the congregation and said, "Took!" Well, that's one way to make a living on loving.

♪

Clay Walker
"If I Could Make A Living"

People who are successful in life are people who do what they love. If you are wondering what to do with your life, ask yourself a very basic question: "What do I love to do?" Or, to get even more basic, ask yourself another question: "What would I even pay people to let me do?" When you know what you really love to do, then you know where you want to direct your life. A wise person once said, "There are no lack of opportunities to make money from what you love doing. There is only the lack of commitment and persistence to make it happen." To put it another way, people spend their whole lives doing something they really don't like because they are afraid of change. In some cases, with bills and family and responsibilities, quitting a present job just in hope of doing something else is not practical. You might want to start by taking small steps to see if you can make money from what you love doing. Do it first as a hobby, or as a part-time job, then see if you can expand it.

When I think of pursuing what we love in life, I'm reminded of the story of a lady who had just cremated her husband, talking to an unmarried friend. The lady said, "Yes, this is the fourth husband I've cremated." Her unmarried friend replied, "Well, life isn't fair. I've never had a husband, and you've got husbands to burn." Well, in life it's not how many or how much of anything that really matters; what counts is that we got something honestly, without deceit.

Aaron Tippin
"I Got It Honest"

All true love is based on honesty and fairness. We want to get what we want honestly, but we also want others to have a chance at the good things of life. That's why love always moves above the romantic commitment to one person to a larger commitment to the rest of society. We want the same good things for others that we would want for our own family. The passion that draws us to one person must also be the passion that leads us to want justice and peace for all people.

The connection between the passionate love of two people for each other, and the passionate commitment to peace and justice for all, is beautifully captured in the Beatitudes of Jesus. Jean Vanier—founder of the "L'Arche communities," homes for people with mental and physical disabilities all over the world—rewrote and expanded the Beatitudes of

Jesus. Vanier's slant on the Beatitudes unfurls as follows:

> Blessed are you because you are gentle; you refuse violence and aggressiveness; you allow yourself to be led by the Spirit into the world of tenderness and patience.
>
> Blessed are you because your heart is pure; you do not accept compromises.
>
> Blessed are you because you are merciful; you attach your heart to the care of others; you will receive mercy and no one will see your sin.
>
> Blessed are you because, at all times and at every moment, you want to be an instrument of peace, seeking unity, understanding, and reconciliation above all things.
>
> Blessed are you because you have allowed your own conscience to develop; you have not been swayed by what people might say about you and have acted as a free individual; you have accepted persecution; you have not been afraid to proclaim the truth. Happy are you who hunger and thirst for what is right. You shall be satisfied.

The Beatitudes challenge us to move beyond the particular commitment of romance and sex between two people to a passionate love commitment that cares about all people. In our selfishness, we want to change people. Love, however, takes people as they are.

Faith Hill
"Take Me As I Am"

The only thing worthy of the name "love" is love that is committed, faithful sexually and romantically to one person, and transferable to all the human race in a common search for peace and justice.

"Love" is the shortest definition of God. St. John wrote that "God is love." Over the course of the centuries, that realization had to be rediscovered again and again. Martin Luther, poring over St. Paul's letter to the Romans, came to realize the overwhelming truth of the doctrine of justification by faith alone. Luther's momentous discovery was that God loved him. Soren Kierkegaard has said that God "becomes the third party in every relationship." The passion of husband and wife reflects the faithful passionate commitment that God has to us.

C.S. Lewis noted that the only proper job of the church, any church, is to bring us closer to God. As Boyd Wright commented, "The buildings, the clergy, the liturgy, the sermons, the good works, all the busy activity, even the Bible itself have at bottom but one purpose—to close the gap so that a single Christian kneeling in prayer can turn to God."

The power of love has the power to heal the divisions within Christianity and within the religions and nations of the world. Fr. Raymond Brown, the world renowned scripture scholar, said, "It is more than embarrassing, it is frightening, to reflect that Christianity was less divided on January 1, 1000, than it may be on January 1, 2000." The only healing for the divisions within religions may not be agreement on all doctrines, but agreement that God is love. As Fr. Andrew Greeley said so well, "The church you belong to is less important than what you believe God meant to reveal through Jesus. The point is to come to the belief that the picture of the universe as a love affair between God and man is not an exaggeration, but an understatement—the only thing that really matters in Catholic Christianity."

Therefore, the power of love is the power to love like

God, to be in love with God, and to love each other the way
we would love God.

Amen.

Lee Roy Parnell
"Power Of The Love"

Also by Father Joe...

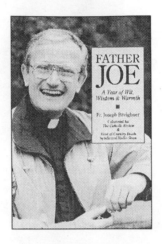

A Year of Wit, Wisdom & Warmth
(ISBN 1-885938-00-4)
214 pp., pbk
$16.95

"With a bottomless store of jokes, anecdotes, parables,
spiritual citations, self-help adages and homespun
homilies, Father Joe Breighner has become a populist
priest, with a congregation that cuts across parish,
generational and class boundaries."
The Baltimore Sun

 To order, call
Cathedral Foundation Press
(410) 547-5324